You are my favorite "Toastie"
and a most talented writer, speaker
and marketer.

Wordapodia
Volume One

Enjoy some laughs and smiles,
and thank you for all of your
advice and support.

Matt Golding

PS Spread the Word-a-pedia
and avoid Vegestarians at all
costs.

ALSO BY THE AUTHOR

So So Wisdom: The Misplaced Teachings of So So Gai

Mixed Emotions

All That Twitters Is Not Goldberg
(coming very soon)

For more information on all writings,
projects, and public appearances
—past, present, and future—
please contact matt@tipofthegoldberg.com
or call Matt directly
856.796.0610

Wordapodia
Volume One

An Encyclopedia
of Real Fake Words

Matthew J. Goldberg

iUniverse, Inc.
New York Bloomington

Wordapodia: Volume One
An Encyclopedia of Real Fake Words

iUniverse books may be ordered through booksellers or by contacting:

iUniverse
1663 Liberty Drive
Bloomington, IN 47403
www.iuniverse.com
1-800-Authors (1-800-288-4677)

ISBN: 978-1-4502-2273-0 (pbk)
ISBN: 978-1-4502-2275-4 (cloth)
ISBN: 978-1-4502-2274-7 (ebk)

Printed in the United States of America

iUniverse rev. date: 8/31/10

Especially for my parents:

Robert J. Goldberg, who still uses the English language so adroitly

and

Sara Passo Goldberg, of blessed memory,
an entertainer and punster
in the very best sense
of those words

Contents

Introknowledgments

Creating my first *Wordapodia* has been an interesting process, and I have been inspired to bring it to you by voices residing both inside and outside my head. Identifying all of these muses' voices is difficult, but I hope that the end result of my listening to and following them is a book that will entertain you. It is my further hope that these wordapods will stay with you and that you will look forward to picking up this book—and future volumes—whenever you need a smile or a laugh. Well, not *every* single time, as I hope you have other sources of amusement as well.

The creative fire that somehow produced this book was ignited very early in my life, as my older brothers (Dan and Josh) and I were born into a family that used/uses words creatively. My mom (of blessed memory), Sara Passo Goldberg, was a natural entertainer—both in local theater as a gifted actress and in day-to-day life as a great storyteller—and punster. My dad, Robert J. Goldberg, has now lost most of his eyesight and hearing but almost none of his ability to master the English language with precision, wit, and aplomb. (It's when he does so with a prune that I worry.)

Years ago, my dad was a proud member and chapter president of the University of Minnesota's Toastmasters International club. I am now an active member of Toastmasters (I don't commute to Minneapolis but attend regularly in Voorhees, New Jersey) and believe that the "Word of the Day"—used at each meeting—may have provided subconscious motivation for this book. And no, I can't confirm that the most common "Word of the Day" at Minnesota Toastmasters meetings is *yabetcha*.

If my parents provided early inspiration (and Mom, I borrowed your "necktureen" and "remutt control"), I also received great support from an eclectic cast of *real* fake characters that started speaking to me as soon as I began to write this book. Like the wordapods themselves, these people could and should exist; indeed, they are experts in their respective fields of study and endeavor.

Among this large group of experts that I met with, I am particularly indebted to Sondra Snoozelman, proud madam of the Booklover's Boredello, for providing insight into that rare but valuable institution. Other ladies who immeasurably added to the contents of this book include Helga Hammerschmidt, world champion of **emroidery**, Clara Heatley, the original **Boob Bird**, and the incredible 6'9" **wintersault** legend, Ludmilla Martin.

The many academics I consulted with include the Amish historian Obadiah Stoltzfus, anthropologist Klaus Schulman, **Pastafari** scholar Tosh Kingsmon, and **Talibanjo** expert Mohammed Al-Valentino. I'd like to offer special thanks to Russian Jewish authority Boris-Yuri Fedorov for his interview—to say nothing of the delicious assortment of golden brown **parking lotkes** that he served me.

My pathway to the absurd was illuminated by so many, including **manurologist** Cletus Clever (although he's not the greatest lunch partner), world-renowned **prognocrastinator** Harry Honto, Dr. Woodrow Thorenson, an eminent **rodentist**, and long-suffering **vegestarian** Mars Greenman. When I last saw Mars, he was mesmerized by a large plate of root vegetables. Mars, I hope you have since been able to move forward with your meal.

In addition to these celebrated experts in their respective fields, I greatly benefited from my access to the dedicated faculty and staff of tiny but prestigious Slippery Slope College. This small, liberal arts school—located in eastern Pennsylvania—educates only thirty-five hundred undergraduate students, yet it offers quite an innovative curriculum that is barely rivaled by the much larger land-grant universities.

Admissions Director Phyllis Inonit granted me access to her brilliant staff, which includes Euripedes Amenides, professor of classic literature, Dr Lisa Efstein, a connoisseur and teacher of **whoreticulture**, and **snorganic chemistry** pioneer Dr. Meg A. Hertz.

Last, but never least, I often leaned on the expertise and wisdom of Dr. Marta Hari, psychologist and author of the scholarly work *Young Head Cases*. Marta, your practical approach to psychology sometimes goes beyond the usual bounds of tough love, yet your inimitable approach has enabled you to build a most successful and lucrative practice. While I wanted to do a question-and-answer interview with you, you expertly took control of our sessions. I hope that you will accept this humble acknowledgment in lieu of payment for our time together.

Translation: stop billing me already!

Words for the Wise
Wordapodia User

This book is meant for the creative word enthusiast, the humorist, and the budding *semantician* (a very recent wordapod) alike. It is also intended for anyone who has a good sense of humor—or anyone who at least tolerates a strong, hyperactive one. So what is a w*ordapod*? Rather than tell you, I am taking a leap of faith that you can easily figure it out from the more than 250 such entries in your new *Wordapodia*. You may notice that some of these wordapods are one-word entries and some are comprised of multiple words. That's okay. As long as the wordapod features creative word play and the ability to inform and entertain, I included it—or will, in future volumes.

In order to both entertain and inform you (*enterform* you?), each wordapod was defined and then explored in a number of different ways. The structure of each and every entry was not identical but was not completely random either. I'd like to think that this eclectic method made for a less predictable and better overall reading experience.

Your new encyclopedia of *real* fake words is designed to appeal to a very broad audience. Wordapods were taken from a variety of fields, although my mind may have taken me (and now, you) down certain paths that I really enjoy. As I am a huge baseball fan, there is a special section of baseball wordapods at the end of this volume. Otherwise, the words are arranged alphabetically and feature a strange brew of new words, fun facts, observations, and interviews from the worlds of academia, anthropology, the arts, food, history, love and sex, mythology, politics, recreation, religion, and zoology.

As this is only volume one, I am sure I did not cover *everything*, but I also did not wish to present you with a skimpy book. I thank you for reading it, and if you would like to contact me with an observation, or request, or perhaps a new wordapod for consideration in future volumes, I encourage you to do so.

Just one warning: For your enjoyment and gentle torture, I have included reviews at the end of most of the chapters. Feel free to either skip the reviews or cheat on them; it's your book.

On to the wordapods!

THE FIRST FIFTY
WORDAPODS

Absolute Monarch Butterfly

Absolute Monarch Butterfly (abbreviated AMB) (n)—a large butterfly noted for its orange-brown wings, its long migrations, and its totalitarian ways

Sample Sentence: An erstwhile lover of butterflies, Simon now avoided the whole species after too many unpleasant run-ins with Absolute Monarch Butterflies over the years.

You Know What ... ?

After nearing extinction in the 1980s, the AMB seems to be making a comeback of sorts, with many recent sightings in Europe and New Zealand. While other forms of butterflies are known to be diplomatic and egalitarian—and there are millions of social butterflies who are quite flirtatious—the Absolute Monarch Butterfly is used to getting its own way and making life difficult for all other animals and humans under its rule. The AMB would not even think about flirting like a social butterfly.

As the late Lord Acton might have said, Monarch Butterflies tend to be corrupt, and Absolute Monarch Butterflies tend to corrupt absolutely.

Alabastard

Alabastard (n)—the illegitimate, pale-skinned son of a dark-skinned mother

Please Note: *Alabasterd* is also a legitimate spelling.

Sample Scenario: Kids can be wonderful, and kids can be mean, and Maurice's neighborhood was no different than most. With his shiny, translucent skin, Maurice was often teased and called an alabastard by the jerks that he always seemed to be surrounded by.

Mastering the Word

The term *alabastard* should only be used:

a. sparingly
b. appropriately
c. never
d. against one's enemies
e. all of the above

AlGorithm

AlGorithm (n)—a tiresome speech about the perils our planet is facing delivered smugly by an overweight former vice president

Please Note: This is a new word that seems to have a very precise definition and limited versatility. However, AlGorithms can be spoken by people other than you-know-who about subjects other than you-know-what.

Sample Scenario: It's hard to endure any more of my history prof's tired AlGorithms on learning from the mistakes of our previous generations. I got his drift the first hundred times.

An Al Gore Trivia Question

Al Gore once roomed with _____ at Harvard.
    a. Bill Clinton
    b. Tommy Lee Jones
    c. Harrison Ford
    d. Tipper Rodham
    e. Mick Jagger

Anglephile

Anglephile (n)—a billiards player who loves to hit shots, including bank shots, at strange angles

b) a person who is always looking to take advantage of another

Please Note: Someone can be an anglephile on the pool table but not one in other aspects of life, and vice versa. Of course, sometimes a person is both. Rudolph "Minnesota Fats" Waldreone Jr., the legendary pool hustler, was one such example.

Sample Sentence: When I play Gordon, the anglephile, I always learn something from his creative play—while I also try to ignore his manipulative monologues.

You Know What ... ?

Billiards historian Willie Greenfelt notes, "In researching pool champions from the last seventy-five years, I would estimate that 82 percent of the champions were anglephiles; the remaining 14 percent just made every single straight shot imaginable."

(Editor's note: math is not Willie's forte.)

Anthropomurphic

Anthropomurphic (adj)—ascribing Irish human form and characteristics to something that is not human, let alone Irish

You Know What ... ?

The greatest example of an artist who specializes in anthropomurphism is an oil painter from Danbury, Connecticut, named Seamus O'Leary. In fact, O'Leary has a devoted cult following that snatches up his moderately priced paintings of groups of dogs and cats engaged in various iconic and heartwarming Irish scenes. I took the opportunity to interview him.

Matt: Seamus, why would someone with such an Italian name be drawn toward Irish culture?

Seamus: Believe it or not, Matt, O'Leary is 100 percent Irish, and Seamus is about 99 percent. What are you t—

Matt: I knew that. Just kidding. So are there many anthropomurphic painters out there?

Seamus: There are about ten of us that I know of. The second best may be a good friend of mine named Guido Baldelli.

Matt: I'll leave that one alone. I was looking at the painting that you titled *Rover McShea Wolfing Down a Hearty Bowl of Mulligan Stew.* Great use of color and emotion. Do you have any other works showing cats and dogs eating Irish food?

Seamus: There are dozens of them, with the most popular being *Sneaking Some Cabbage into Church.* My priest had a problem with that one at first, but it's now hanging proudly in his office. He also promised to buy my *Bruno and Toonsie Fighting over a Guiness,* as well as *The Celtic Cats Play a Rousing Number. Guiness* took me years to capture, and I was spiritually exhausted for months after completing it.

Matt: I didn't realize that your work was so exhausting. So what is that painting I see now on your easel? I'm no art critic, but it looks like you have a cat and dog spinning around, kicking their feet up, awhirl in a splash of vibrant colors.

Seamus: It's tentatively titled *Fido and Tabby Dancing a Hard Jig.* I'm awfully proud of that one, and it's just a few brushstrokes from completion.

Anti-somatic

Anti-somatic (adj)—relating to activities that are very harmful to one's body, whether or not they are done intentionally

Observation:

Statistics seem to bear out the very sobering fact that anti-somatism appears to be on the rise today. It's a matter of conjecture why this is so. Do ignorance and laziness trump common sense and easy access to information about how to achieve a healthy lifestyle? Sadly, this would appear to be the case.

Sample Scenario: When I accused Mordechai of being anti-somatic, he thought I was crazy. I then explained the word and pointed out that he drank tons of cheap wine, exercised ten minutes every month, and never slept. Mordechai thought about it, pulled a cigarette from his pocket, and said, "Yeah, so what?"

Aquitic

Aquitic (n)—originally, someone who quits taking swimming lessons; it also may now apply to a swim team member who quits during the season

b) (adj)—of, or relating to, a lack of enthusiasm for swimming

You Know What ... ?

A 2009 survey published in *Sink or Swim Daily* showed that aquitic behavior—based on the number of kids who quit the swim team each year—is at an all-time high. At the same time, a greater percentage of the country's youth now swims than ever before. This leads me to believe that the desire to be an aquitic increases as one gets older.

Sample Sentence: Coach Slippermaker, still reeling from having experienced his top three swimmers leaving the team one month earlier, knew that his team would have won the title if it weren't for all of his aquitics.

Please Note: Swimmers who are suspended from a team are not considered to be aquitics. They may be poor students, cheaters, or partyers, but at least they can hold their heads high: they're *not* aquitics.

Arachnonism

Arachnonism (n)—the act of referring to a spider in such a way that it is not placed in its correct historical context

Sample Scenario: I overheard Peter speaking to a friend about the original *Spiderman* movie as if it hadn't been released yet. Butting into the conversation, I accused him of using an arachnonism.

You Know What ... ?

In a preliminary review of this book by a marketing group, arachnonism had three interesting distinctions:

- 85 percent found it to be one of the three hardest words to use in a sentence
- 54 percent found it to be the most difficult word to pronounce
- 5 percent couldn't even find the entry

Arbihairy

Arbihairy (adj)—characterized by an uncontrolled, unreasonable, or erratic amount of hair

Please Note: This may refer to any type of hair—whether facial hair, scalp hair, body hair, or hair in some other location.

Sample Scenario: When I saw my reflection in my car window, I looked so arbihairy. There was, seemingly, just a tuft or two of hair on top of my head and then what looked like a mullet shooting down the back of my neck.

You Know What ... ?

Rafael Cortino, proprietor of Corty Coiffs Men's Hair Salon of Parsnippany. New Jersey, related this about his business. "We give any type of cut the customer asks for. It can be anything from a traditional business cut to a back-to-school special, a crew, a buzz, a cue-ball, an eight-ball, or something even more arbihairy. It doesn't matter to me, as long as they pay for it. I don't have to wear the thing."

Asiten

Asiten (adj)—something so utterly unintelligent and ridiculous that the word asinine doesn't do it justice

Please Note: Although some **stupometers** (please see entry) are said to go all the way to asi-11, more empirical evidence is needed to accept this as a new word.

Sample Scenario: Perhaps the vice-presidential debate was the last straw, or maybe it was the Katie Couric interview. It may have even been when Sarah Palin quit as governor of Alaska. Whatever the case, Marge had seen and heard enough and was moved to say, "If I have to listen to Sarah Palin's asiten comments one more time, I'm going to smash my fifty-two-inch TV to smithereens."

Ass-steroid

Ass-steroid (n)—a performance-enhancing substance administered via a syringe in the buttocks

(What were you expecting, anyway?)

Sample Sentence: It became quite apparent to his students that muscle-bound, temperamental Professor Irejuice was more interested in ass-steroids than asteroids.

Observation:

I am a huge baseball fan, as are many of my friends. We have had quite a few discussions about the problem with steroids in Major League Baseball and how it's affecting perception of the integrity of the game.

When I mentioned the word "ass-steroids," my friend, Eric, put it best: "It doesn't matter where they take the syringe; it's the fans who get it in the end."

Assmatic

Assmatic (noun)—a person suffering from assma, a condition marked by the ability to both breathe and talk almost exclusively from one's backside

(adj)—describing a condition marked by the unique ability to breathe and talk almost exclusively from one's backside

Sample Sentence: In light of the three packs of cigarettes Jimmy smoked daily—and all of the useless drivel he constantly spewed—I told him that he had a good chance of being both an asthmatic and an assmatic. Oddly, he wasn't thrilled with my prediction.

You Know What ... ?

While it is estimated that roughly 8 percent of all Americans suffer from asthma, there is no such data available on assmatics. My supposition is that at least 50 percent of all Americans are exposed to assmatics on at least a weekly basis. The effects are somewhat similar to those of second-hand smoke: coughing, nausea, and a reduced quality of life.

Bananadanna

Bananadanna (n)—a large scarf fashioned from banana peels typically worn on the forehead or around the neck

Sample Sentence: The motorcycle gang looked quite intimidating, especially when we caught sight of the bananadannas worn haughtily by their biker chicks.

You Know What ... ?

According to research conducted by the prestigious WOBOT (Women on Bikes of Texas) Institute, only 22.3 percent of all women who identify with an outlaw motorcycle gang admit to regularly wearing a bananadanna during rides. Of the remaining 77.7 percent, at least 25 percent have tried it only once but cited "unappealing scent" and "bad reaction by their partners" as key factors in not continuing the practice.

Barkolepsy

Barkolepsy (n)—a condition afflicting dogs with the sudden and repeated urgency to sleep

Sample Sentence: Although my beloved old cocker spaniel, Buff, suffered from epilepsy, I thought the disease to be preferable to my Doberman's barkolepsy.

You Know What ... ?

Barkoleptics Anonymous estimated that the top ten canine breeds complaining of barkolepsy (no, they don't yet offer a twelve-step program) in 2008 were:

- Airedale Terrier
- Doberman Pinscher
- Welsh Corgi
- Chihuahua
- Australian Shepherd
- Cocker Spaniel
- Bulldog
- Golden Recliner
- Miniature Schnoozer
- Lousy Napso

Barrabuddah

Barrabuddah (n)—a fat, tropical (and highly spiritual) fish that eats nothing but vegetables

Observation:

As of now, barrabuddah only denotes fish with these qualities. By the next edition, it may refer to certain lawyers, financial advisors, and insurance salesmen as well.

Sample Scenario:

Joan was very proud of her little goldfish and would both feed and admire them at least twice a day. But her roommate, Charmaine, was always full of surprises. Joan returned to her apartment one night only to find that her goldfish had been flushed down the toilet and replaced with three shiny barrabuddahs. She thought about strangling Charmaine, but after getting to know the new fish, she became quite serene and soon even gave up eating meat and chicken.

Barry White-fish Salad

Barry White-fish Salad (n)—a plate of sturgeon, herring, whiting, and the like eaten while listening to deep-voiced, romantic music

You Know What ... ?

In most common usage, a Barry White-fish salad (or, simply "some *Barry Whitefish*") refers to a social gathering of African Americans and Jews where a fish platter is enjoyed. These seem to be especially popular in New York City and Santa Fe, New Mexico.

Sample Sentence: Having no plans for the weekend, I was extremely psyched when Latisha invited me over for some Barry Whitefish.

Warning:

A Barry Manilow-fish Salad has a totally different vibe and doesn't have much appeal to African Americans (or many Jews with good taste for that matter).

Bedouin and Breakfast

Bedouin and Breakfast (n)—a hospitality tent set up by nomadic Arabs, who greet their fellow wanderers with water, pita, and a good night's sleep—all at a very good price

You Know What ... ?

The Bedouins are mostly Arabic-speaking and are found in the Middle East, where they recently were said to comprise about 10 percent of the population. (Since they're usually in motion, it's hard to get a more accurate head count.)

Most Bedouins live a primitive lifestyle, with sheep- and camel-breeding being their main livelihoods. Some of these proud tribesmen do run Bedouin and Breakfast joints; the most famous franchise among them is called Tent 6. Their very ingenious slogan is, "If we had lights, we'd gladly leave them on for you."

Please Note: The middle letters of *hospitality* are *p-i-t-a*. Is this just a coincidence? Much as I'd like to think that the words are related, I can find no etymological nexus. But that's okay; I just had the great pleasure of writing "etymological nexus."

Benefriction

Benefriction (n)—the closing address of a religious service that manages to piss off the assembled body

Observation:

Reverend Michael Golightly, editor of *This Weak Sermon,* authored a fine piece about benefrictions in his February 2009 issue. Golightly asserts: "The benefriction, while a controversial type of address (whether issued in churches, synagogues, or mosques), does have its adherents. Even though it makes people angry, it comes after the plate has already been passed and the donations are already in. Even more to the good, most of those who storm off manage to return the following week and even bring a new friend or family member with them just to see what may be spewed forth from the pulpit."

Sample Sentence: Father Metrano always conducted a beautiful service, but he could also be counted on to recite a benefriction that had his parishioners almost coming to blows in the pews.

Biknockerlars

Biknockerlars (n)—glasses that help guys zero in on women's chests

You Know What ... ?

Vince Raputo has sold a biknockerlar or two in the twenty-five years that he has owned and operated Vinnie's Visions, a specialty optical shop in Philadelphia. He agreed to an interview, which is excerpted below.

Matt: I am told that you are a descendant of a very famous person or two from your native Italy. Who would they be?

Vince: Most of your readers have, no doubt, heard of Galileo Galilei. He's a great, great, great, uncle of mine. Did you know that his real name was Galileo di Vincenzo Bonaiuti de' Galilei? He was known as the "father of modern science," and among other things, he popularized the use of the telescope. Now, you may not have heard of his brother.

Matt: Can't say I have.

Vince: It is said that binoculars are a distant, or maybe close, cousin of the telescope, and their invention is attributed to his brother. By the way, the binocular begat the first biknockerlar, and there's a good story attached to it.

Matt: Please share.

Vince: Garibaldi Patrezia Bonito Romano de' Galelei, known to his friends as Garry G, adapted his brother's device, as he professed to wish to get a better view of the opera. Taking advantage of this unique technology, his mini-telescopes were invariably trained on the gorgeous Italian ladies in the luxury boxes—not on the stage. This, logically enough, soon set the stage for the invention of the biknockerlars, a device enjoyed quite frequently by concertgoers and sports fans.

Matt: Wow, a man after my own heart. What a guy.

Vince: Our family's quite proud. Garry G was a true Renaissance man. The man had vision.

Bilkshake

Bilkshake (n)—a very expensive beverage

Sample Scenario: I love the local ice cream store, but if I pass on their strawberry bilkshake, I can get almost the same quality milkshake for half the price at a fast food restaurant.

You Know What ... ?

A bilkshake does not have to be an overpriced milkshake, as the term refers to any overpriced beverage. Per a recent study conducted by the renowned Slurp Foundation, the five leading types of bilkshakes were found to be:

- Imported beers
- Milkshakes
- Bottled water
- Orange juice
- Eggnog

Blink Verse

Blink Verse (n)—unrhymed poetry written in such a bizarre fashion that it makes your eyes blink rapidly when reading it

Sample Scenario:

Larry and Rose, two poetry enthusiasts, enjoyed going together to the monthly "Open Mic Night" at their local bookstore. One Tuesday evening, a steady stream of poorly prepared poets took the stage, and they never connected with their audience. Being unable to sit through any more of the proceedings, Larry yelled out, "This blink verse royally sucks," and stormed over to the coffee shop. (A couple of the other attendees followed him to the coffee shop and praised him for reciting the best free-form poem of the night.)

Observation:

All art is very subjective, and perhaps poetry is even more so. Remember that one man's blink verse is another man's masterpiece.

Blubbergasted

Blubbergasted (**v**)—dumbstruck, as if hit by a lightning bolt, when one discovers how much one weighs

Sample Scenario: I had been dieting every day for about two weeks but had steadfastly refused to step on the bathroom scale during that time. Convinced that my jeans now felt a little looser, I happily climbed onto my scale. Well, you guessed it; I was blubbergasted to discover that I had gained six pounds.

You Know What ... ?

Although countries such as the United States have a greater percentage of overweight individuals, Australia was found to have the highest percentage of blubbergasted people. Reliable sources tell me that most of those blubbergasted Aussies have been known to talk back to their scales, saying things like, "Bollocks. Got to ease off the lollies and grog, matey."

Blubberneck

Blubberneck (v)—to crane one's neck to stare at something or someone who is really fat

Blubbernecking (n)—the act of quickly turning one's neck while on a whale-watching expedition

You Know What ... ?

In the 1950s, *blubbernecking* referred to the activity of two fat people engaged in passionate smooching, usually while in a parked car.

Sample Scenario: George and Wilma Ronaldson had been very excited to go on their annual whale watching expedition, but their voyage did not work out as planned. The weather was cold and wet, and four hours into it, they had seen nothing of any consequence. Wilma complained, "You know, George, I killed my shoulder doing all that blubbernecking, and all I saw were some Frisbees and beach balls."

Boredello

Boredello (n)—an unusual institution in which female librarians are paid to read to their (mostly) male clients until they fall asleep

Sample Sentence: Ruprecht's insomnia came to be costly, as he made frequent stops to the boredello to get a proper night's sleep.

You Know What ... ?

I spoke to Sondra Snoozelman, who is the madam of the Booklover's Boredello, a fine institution in Cherry Hill, New Jersey.

Matt: Sondra, I don't know too much about boredellos. How many are there in the United States?

Sondra: From what I've read, there are seventeen legal boredellos in the United States. To this point, all are in the states of New Jersey and Montana.

Matt: Fascinating. Who are your clientele, and what is their minimum age?

Sondra: In New Jersey, you must be at least eighteen—seventeen if you have a note from a doctor or legal guardian. Our clientele is very diverse, from politicians to professional athletes to the homeless.

Matt: What do you call the women you employ, and what qualities do you look for in a, um, bookstitute?

Sondra: Bookstitute? Not bad. We don't really have any name other than Boredello Babes. I look for someone who is well read, has a soothing voice, can work flexible hours, and is not so attractive that she will keep clientele up all night reading.

Matt: What type of fees does a Boredello Babe command?

Sondra: Generally, we charge between $20 and $30 per hour (they get a fifty/fifty split with me), plus tips. Quite reasonable, especially if your health insurance picks up 80 percent of the tab, not counting the gratuity, of course.

Matt: Two more questions, Sondra. Do *you* still read to clientele, and what books do you recommend?

Sondra: Yes, I'll sometimes pinch-read, and no, I won't divulge any of my secrets.

Boroform

Boroform (n)—any speech or event that bores and/or annoys someone to the point of paralysis

Sample Sentence: I tried to watch the political debate, but the deadly dull exchanges served as a kind of boroform.

Mastering the Word

Which of the following—given the above definition—would you consider to be the most powerful type of boroform for/on you?

- Political debate
- College lecture
- Romantic comedy
- Auto racing
- Bowling
- Yard work
- Shopping
- Talking with your spouse
- Reality TV show
- Your job

Braggadocent

Braggadocent (n)—a museum or tour guide who is overly proud and boastful of his/her abilities

Sample Sentence: Although Leonard was certainly a knowledgeable guide for the Philadelphia Art Museum, he was such a braggadocent that his tours became insufferable.

Observation:

In my experience, a good docent can make or break the whole museum experience. A great docent brings paintings and artifacts alive with his love and enthusiasm for the subject. A good docent does the same to a lesser extent, and even a decent docent can enhance the experience slightly.

Then there are the poor docents and the qualified, but arrogant, braggadocents. I have had a few of the latter and soon wished I had gone on the self-guided tours, even if I knew nothing about what I was viewing. And I won't even mention *The Dirty Docents*. Oops!

Braillehouse

Braillehouse (n)—a special jailhouse building designed for legally blind inmates

You Know What ... ?

The legally blind population is one of the most law-abiding demographics in the United States. Consequently, there has not been much of a need for braillehouses in this country.

But the first (and apparently only) braillehouse in this country was built in Kansas after complaints by inmate George "Deadeye" Bostich that conditions in the notorious Leavenworth Prison discriminated against the blind. Deadeye, who was doing a twenty-year stretch for a slew of petty crimes, was able to convene a special public hearing before the Kansas Penal Board, which set the motion for a beautiful, state-of-the-art, forty-acre corrections facility in Kansas City.

Very sadly, Bostich never got to see (no pun intended) his new residence come to fruition. Three days before he was to cut the ribbon at the dedication ceremony, Deadeye died suddenly at the tender age of 113. Foul play was not ruled out.

Brewp

Brewp (n)—a disgusting, almost inedible soup-like concoction

(v)—to regurgitate on something or someone, as in: "The pigeons brewped all over my brand-new red sports car."

You Know What ... ?

As legend has it, the original brewp was something dreamed up by a Milwaukee tavern owner named Gunter Brout, who got hammered and boiled together a fifty/fifty mixture of beer and his popular chicken dumpling soup.

Calling it brewp, he marketed it to his regulars, with this slogan:

You crave our beer
You like our soup
You'll really, really
Love our brewp.

When he proudly ladled out free samples to his faithful, only two of the approximately twenty-five patrons asked for more, and they did so (presumably) on a bet.

That was, effectively, the end of brewp as a menu item at the Brout Tavern, but the legend was just beginning. Some local wags termed brewp "the soup that made Milwaukee infamous."

Buddahful

Buddahful (adj)—very attractive and zaftig-plus, if somewhat overweight. It can refer to men or women of all ages.

Sample Scenario: Heidi had been on quite a few dates, blind and sighted alike, and tended to be quite fussy about taking on any of these projects as boyfriends. When I asked Heidi about her latest blind date, she replied that Gunnar was a buddahful person, both inside and out.

Mastering the Word

The word *buddahful* connotes (to you):
- a very spiritual person
- a beautiful, if overweight, gem
- your idea of a great person
- all of the above
- none of the above

Canbankerous

Canbankerous (adj)—of, or relating to, an ornery employee of a financial institution

Sample Sentence: With my favorite teller on vacation, I knew that I would be waited on by the ever-canbankerous Rusty.

Observation:

I surveyed all of the coauthors of this book to get their responses to the following question: "What makes for a friendly (non-canbankerous) bank employee?" Top factors cited were:

1. Nice smile and gracious attitude
2. Remembering my name or something about me
3. Ability to make the occasional bank-error-in-my-favor
4. Gives me free lollipops
5. Prompt service

Cankersaurus

Cankersaurus (n)—an extinct herbivorous reptile of the Jurassic Period that suffered from extremely painful ulcers around the mouth

You Know What ... ?

Research into this strange creature is relatively new, as scientists have been wary of publishing findings on Cankersaurus. Afraid of perpetrating a hoax on the order of "Piltdown Man," they have proceeded with some caution.

Paleontologists have, however, hypothesized the following about Cankersaurus:

- He/she lived mostly in what is now Columbus, Ohio, but enjoyed a weekend excursion to Kentucky every now and then.
- He/she was a contemporary of Brontosaurus, though they rarely socialized or had dinner together.
- A fully grown Cankersaurus weighed about twenty-three metric tons but was surprisingly light on its feet.
- Cankersaurus was almost sixty-eight feet long (slightly shorter than Brontosaurus), but was known for being even fiercer and for having a temper caused by bad meals and even worse breath.
- This strange dinosaur had five legs, making it the only known quintopod of the Jurassic Period.
- Why did it become extinct even before the other dinosaurs? Scientists have posited the theory that its prominent, sometimes hideous, canker sores discouraged second dates— let alone activities that might have led to procreation.

Sample Sentence: My lack of sleep and penchant for eating tons of oranges had me feeling like a miniature Cankersaurus.

Cannabus

Cannabus (n)—a large, commercial motor vehicle that allows its passengers to smoke marijuana legally

Please Note: Although many a school bus may seem (and smell) like a cannabus, they are not truly cannabuses, as smoking pot is not legal there. It's just tolerated.

You Know What ... ?

There were many more cannabuses during the 1960s and 1970s, when large charter services such as Rolling Doobies thrived and recorded all-time high profits. Sadly, the Reagan administration (as well as changes in the auto industry) had effectively put an end to such services by the 1980s.

The only existing cannabus company that we are aware of is called Greybong. They advertise deluxe "roach" seats, and their unofficial motto is: "Go Greybong, and leave the smoking to us."

Cannibal Lectern

Cannibal Lectern (n)—a reading desk or speaker's stand used by people who eat human flesh

You Know What ... ?

Cannibals have, in my opinion, been rightfully stigmatized for their barbaric, anti-social, deviant behavior. However, research has shown that many practitioners of this ghastly habit are some of the finest, most literate people on earth.

In fact, cannibal lecterns are still being manufactured to accommodate cannibals who give speeches, lectures, and poetry readings in a small number of bookstores and libraries in the United States.

Sample Sentence: Whenever I give a book reading on an empty stomach, I fear that they'll set me up with a cannibal lectern, causing me to look at my audience in a whole new way.

Cantelope

Cantelope (n)—one who believes in a traditional wedding—at all costs

You Know What ... ?

(According to www.costofwedding.com)
The average cost of a wedding is just over $20,000, and that *does not include* small items like the engagement ring and the honeymoon.

Not a tiny bit of change, when one considers that the average marriage lasts between eight and nine years.

Sample Sentence: Rosie couldn't wait to jet off to Vegas with her beloved, but alas, Filbert was a dyed-in-the-wool cantelope.

Observation:

That doesn't make Filbert a fruit. A nut, perhaps?

CARdiac

CARdiac (n)—a heart attack that occurs while in a moving vehicle

Sample Sentence: While flipping another driver the bird with gusto, poor Sherman suffered a CARdiac.

Please Note: *CARdiac* is one of very few words (in any known human language) that capitalize only its first three letters.

Warning:

CARDiac, denoting a coronary disease suffered while playing pinochle, bridge, or Old Maid, is not yet recognized as a new wordapod, but because of the high and growing number of such unfortunate incidents, it may make our next edition.

Cargantuan

Cargantuan (adj)—enormous, used almost exclusively to describe a motor vehicle

Sample Scenario: Uma loved to drive her white Hummer, even on the shortest of trips. Her good fortune was that her cargantuan vehicle got pretty good gas mileage.

Please Note: The above was not intended as a free plug.

Observation:

Cargantuan hummer (lower case) may also refer to an activity that may be enjoyed in a moving vehicle.

Caribooster Seat

Caribooster Seat or Caribooster Chair (n)—a very large padded chair used to keep baby deer (or reindeer) safe and secure while feeding

You Know What ... ?

Caribou, the name given to the North American wild reindeer, are in danger of extinction, as many of their herds are thinning out. This is not good news for nature lovers, nor for Caribox, the world's largest manufacturer of caribooster seats.

Caribox spokesperson Peg Granso lamented, "We have had to lay off some of our best workers, as sales have declined steadily the last twenty-two years or so. On the bright side, the average size of a newborn baby is increasing every year, so you never know."

Sample Sentence: Jenna joked that her baby, Brutus, had gotten so large that she would have to feed him in a caribooster seat.

Carnibore

Carnibore (n)—someone incapable of talking about anything else but meat

Please Note: A **carnisnore** is someone who *dreams* exclusively about meat.

Sample Scenario: Ralph had always done his Sunday grocery shopping at Lou's Corner Market. That changed as he came to the realization that Butcher Bob was too much the carnibore for his tastes. Instead, he started going to the big supermarket near the mall, where he could grab his meat while enjoying a quick chat about the economy.

Mastering the Word

Carnibore and *Carnisnore* are:
   a. synonymous
   b. mutually exclusive
   c. related, in that a carnisnore is an extreme carnibore
   d. linked: a carnibore can be a carnisnore, and vice versa, but there is no direct correlation.

Carpool Tunnel Syndrome

Carpool Tunnel Syndrome (n)—a pattern of boredom and psychological pain caused by too many trips with the same coworkers to and from work

You Know What ... ?

Seeking more information about carpool tunnel syndrome, I contacted my friend, psychiatrist Lorenz Raziki, who sat down for a quick chat.

Matt: We have been told that carpooling is great for the environment, so what's the problem with it?

Dr. Raziki: Carpooling may take a few cars off the road, but at what price? It is estimated that almost twelve billion dollars of productivity is lost from the American economy each year due to the effects of carpool tunnel syndrome.

Matt: What are some of the effects, and shouldn't the environment be priority number one?

Dr. Raziki: Carpooling may, indeed, be good for the environment, but we are seeing many deleterious psychological and physiological effects from the policy of enforced carpooling that have led to many physical, mental, and psychological disorders.

Matt: I still don't get it, Doc. What about the happy mental picture I have of sharing the driving duties and forestalling the loneliness of the road?

Dr. Raziki: Yes, that is the propaganda associated with carpooling, but the reality is that carpool tunnel syndrome is serious.

Matt: Tell me more. To be indelicate, I think this is just an excuse for people to skip work.

Dr. Raziki: Not so. How about all the extra conversations about work, not being able to play your own music, and sitting on the trash left by your coworkers' kids? Still think it's funny? Carpool tunnel syndrome is no joke.

Matt: I stand corrected. Is there anything else you'd like to add?

Dr. Raziki: Maybe another time. One of my colleagues has to be home by 5:30, and it's my turn to drive.

Carrion Luggage

Carrion Luggage (n)—special luggage designed to carry and deodorize decaying flesh, thus appearing to meet airline standards for what can come aboard

Observation:

In an era where airline safety and counterterrorism security measures are of paramount importance, it is not recommended that one bring decaying flesh aboard a plane—even if one has the best carrion luggage on the market.

Having said that, while good carrion luggage is hard to find, many specialty stores will discount these bags during the winter. Most carrion luggage sets also offer a nice array of colors and styles. Just yesterday, I ran across an ad for a lovely American Shlepper carrion luggage set that said it was "good for handling everything from a killer cardigan to a killed carcass."

Carrotocracy

Carrotocracy (n)—an unusual political system in which people possessing the biggest carrots are rewarded with power and fame

You Know What ... ?

Researching a ton of world political history, I could not find any evidence of an actual carrotocracy. Meredith Larson, author of the excellent book, *Suburban Legends: Far and Wide*, did note the following:

"In the fourth century BC, in a land mass now known as Slovenia, there existed a carrotocracy that was run by farmer Slavoj Hanoj. Alleged to possess the biggest carrots in town, he and his fellow farmers were put in charge of all phases of the kingdom's economic, domestic, and international affairs—such as they were at the time.

"The experimental government proved to be disastrous, and Hanoj and his cronies soon lost control. They were done in by a hostile coup led by a bunch of snowman impersonators. Some of these militant revolutionaries may have even been male porn stars."

Catastropic

Catastropic (adj)—of, or relating to, a disastrous vacation in a warm weather spot

Sample Sentence: Happy to kiss American soil after two horrid weeks in Acapulco, I tried to put the whole catastropic experience behind me.

Mastering the Word

Which of the following factors would most likely cause *you* to have a catastropic experience?

- Bad weather
- Excessive cost
- Sunburn
- Terrible food and drink options
- Lost luggage
- Member of traveling party drowning
- Annoying cruise mates
- Gastrointestinal complications
- Inability to speak to the natives

Caterer-waul

Caterer-waul (v)—to shriek and wail like a wounded cat after getting an invoice from the caterer

Sample Sentence: My friend Steven is normally a pretty cool customer, but he caterer-wauled like a castrated feline when he got the bill for his daughter's wedding reception.

Observation:

The recent spate of caterer-wauling incidents is attributable to at least three factors:

a. the very high cost of paying for lavish affairs
b. the lack of budgeting by those sponsoring such affairs
c. poor math skills on the part of the sponsors.

My friend, Joanie Goutrageous, of Come to Us Only Catering (I'm trying to get her to change the name of her business, to say nothing of her own last name.) mentioned to us, "While weddings and other parties are not cheap, we always itemize, and stick to, the initial costs we present. Still, I can always expect someone in the party to caterer-waul like a frightened baby hamster."

Chairismatic

Chairismatic (adj)—of, or relating to, the quality of being quite at home in a recliner

Observation:

How and why is it that both of the following trends seem to be on the upswing?

- More people are exercising than ever before in countless different ways.
- There are more overweight and more obese Americans than ever before.

One of the reasons may be our careless, unhealthful diets. Another reason may be our love for reclining chairs and sofas—the venue where lots of those empty calories are consumed.

To be clear, a chairismatic person does not need to be overweight, though it doesn't hurt any. The "chairisma" comes more from the way in which that person carries (or does not choose to carry) himself.

Sample Sentence: Before sitting down on the new sofa, I waited for my chairismatic hostess, Katrina, to lead the way.

Challahlujah

Challahlujah (int; n)—an exclamation of joy and praise in reaction to eating a delicious piece of braided bread

You Know What ... ?

Many people may know challah as that yellowish bread that makes for great French toast, and there's certainly nothing wrong with that. In fact, quite a few people informally surveyed mentioned to me that leftover challah (often mispronounced, but in pronouncing the "ch," you *should* strain your throat and expel some saliva) makes for their favorite type of French toast.

Challah is the traditionally braided (egg) bread eaten by Jews on Friday night and Saturday mornings, as well as on the eve and the day of other holidays. Be it round or long, seeded or plain, a well-baked challah is a thing of beauty and often has me screaming, "Challahlujah, praise the Lord ... and don't forget the lovely person who baked it."

Sample Scenario: Rabbi Irv Meyersberg was hosting a very nice Friday night (Shabbat) dinner, when his wife, Rivka, brought out two of the most beautiful sesame-seed challahs they had ever seen. After blessing it, their hot daughter, Chana, took one bite and exclaimed, "Challahlujah" in an almost orgasmic fashion. Needless to say, Rabbi Meyersberg shot her an icy look of great disapproval.

(Also needless to say, she was sent to bed without any hamantashen.)

Champainful

Champainful (adj)—relating to a burning feeling caused by too much bubbly in the eyes

Observation:

We've all seen the celebrations when the champagne corks are popped and the bubbly flows freely. Depending upon the occasion, either the top-shelf stuff is used or some cheap substitute like sparkling apple cider is substituted. In any event, getting one's eyes immersed in that bubbly stuff can be somewhat champainful. I'm not really the expert here: my very few personal sports championships were always celebrated with beer and wings. Now, when the hot sauce from the wings hit my eyes ...

Mastering the Word

All-time NBA greats Michael Jordan (six world championships) and Bill Russell (eleven titles) must have had many champainful moments.

Chimpansy

Chimpansy (n)—derogatory slang for an effeminate male who facially resembles an ape

Sample Scenario: Davey was a big kid with a face like a primate, but his appearance belied his gentle nature. He knew that life, and the neighborhood toughs, treated him unfairly. "Just because I look like a gorilla but prefer to play with dolls, that doesn't mean that I'm a chimpansy," complained Davey—to anyone who would listen.

Observation:

I know what you're thinking. It's difficult enough to grow up as a big, gentle, effeminate boy in a sometimes cruel society. And then there are those wise guys (like the author of this very book) who come up with these nicknames. In my own defense, I will ask all of you kind readers to get permission before calling someone a chimpansy.

Chocolate Chipshot

Chocolate Chipshot (n)—in golf, a marvelously played pitch or chip shot that finds its way into the hole

You Know What ... ?

The term *chocolate chipshot* was recently coined by amateur golfer (and unpaid instructor) Duffer McPurdy. He explained that his short game is so poor that holing out a chip shot *tastes* extra sweet.

Chocolate chipshots are often the result of luck just as much as they are the residue of preparation and skill. But whatever the case, they do feel and taste sweet. Yours truly, a decent athlete but terrible golfer, has enjoyed one or two of these (98 percent luck in my case), and have also witnessed PGA tourneys won because of a chocolate chipshot (usually 40–60 percent luck for even the pros).

Sample Sentence: While usually an excellent sport, Newman walked off the course with a cursory handshake and a look of disgust after his opponent threw in an improbable chocolate chipshot on the eighteenth hole to steal the tournament.

Clausetrophobia

Clausetrophobia (n)—a great (and totally rational) fear of legal documents and legalese

Warning: If you are suffering from an acute case of clausetrophobia, you may want to avoid reading the following—even if you agree with the sentiments.

> **Whereas,** I (known as the party of the first part) have read many and various and sundry, at least one million (1,000,000) documents, of legal tender from parties of the second (2nd) and third (3rd) parts, and

> **Whereas,** my eyes (the organs most responsible for the first party's sight) and my head (cranium and environs) have been exposed to thousands (1000s) of headaches from perusing and reading said legal documents outlined above in the preceding paragraph, and

> **Whereas,** the party of the first part (I) believe that many of you (parties of the second part) can identify, ratify, and find resonance and meaning in this observation, then,

> **Pursuant** to these events, I (the party of the first part) endeavor to posit and place under consideration for this book (that, hopefully, parties from many parts have purchased and are enjoying) the word "clausetrophobia" to describe the phenomenon of wishing to avert writing run-on drivel such as the party of the first part (I) is engaging in right now.

Okay, the party of the first part feels a lot better now.

Clockenspiel

Clockenspiel (n)—orchestral bells equipped with two hammers and a timepiece

Warning:

Some spell this unusual instrument "clockenshpiel," but technically they're incorrect, so they should stop this practice at once!

You Know What ... ?

The glockenspiel (a clockenspiel without the clock) is utilized on everything from classical pieces by Mozart to military and marching band songs. On a clockenspiel, the timepiece element helps to keep the bells in perfect rhythm and also makes sure that the sometimes tedious concerts don't drag on too long.

Sample Sentence: Hans played his clockenspiel with great exuberance and perfect timing, allowing the audience to bask in the brilliance of his orchestra's rendition of "Old MacDonald Had a Farm."

REVIEW OF FIRST FIFTY

1. Rachel's golden retriever keeps falling asleep at the weirdest times. It may very well be suffering from:
    a. benefriction
    b. ass-steroids
    c. assma
    d. barkolepsy
Okay, that's the last freebie.

2. The Council on African American and Jewish Cooperation released a paper saying that there would be more cohesion between the two groups if they sat down together more frequently for:
    a. bilkshakes
    b. Barry White-fish Salad
    c. chocolate chipshots
    d. brewp
    e. all of the above

3. Which of these items would most commonly be found in the stands at an NFL game?
    a. boroform
    b. bananadannas
    c. braggadocents
    d. biknockerlars

4. Reduced productivity and irritability may be signs of:
    a. clausetrophobia
    b. carpool tunnel syndrome
    c. too many ass-steroids
    d. all of the above
    e. a and b only

COLLIDOSCOPIC
LEFTIES

Collidoscope

Collidoscope (n)—a psychedelic, tube-shaped instrument used to enhance the viewing of traffic accidents

Sample Scenario: Hank and Tommy were a couple of college freshmen with a lack of direction in their lives. Their favorite shared pastime was getting high on life and then taking their collidoscopes with them to the highway overpass.

You Know What ... ?

Collidoscopes, because of their controversial purpose, have been banned from purchase in most states. These states evidently feel that collidoscopes encourage accidents—or at the very least, promote the feeling that driving is not to be taken seriously.

Ruben Johnson, president of Cool Scopes, Ltd., a leading manufacturer of collidoscopes, begs to differ. "Accidents will always happen," he says. "We just add a little color to the experience." So far, only New Jersey, Ohio, and Alaska agree with Johnson.

Columnbine

Columnbine (v)—to merge together two unrelated columns into one unifying one

b) to merge together two data columns on an Excel spreadsheet

Sample Scenario: Bob Briggs was quite the procrastinator, and he once again found himself right up against the deadline for submitting his column. He had two ideas, but he didn't have enough material to complete either. The first was about his experiences with social networking sites, and the second was about the clash between nudity and modesty in the nineteenth century. Bob ended up columnbining the two ideas into one piece titled "Naked Social Networking in the 1800s."

Was it successful? I'm not sure, but he did kill one bird with two stones.

Sample Sentence: I am grateful to my colleague, Buena, for showing me how to columnbine data on my spreadsheets.

Conventory

Conventory (n)—a complete listing of the amount of nuns (formerly a list of the total number of monks, friars, and nuns) living in a particular convent

You Know What ... ?

The conventory is a fairly recent phenomenon that I just became aware of. I spoke with Hilda McLune, author of the illuminating new book, *Nuns on the Run: Creatures of Habit* to find out more.

Matt: Hilda, when were the first conventories utilized?

Hilda: They appear to date back to the 1950s, due to the exploits of Sister Marie Pellegrino.

Matt: What can you tell our readers about her?

Hilda: Sister Marie "Sweet Feet" Pellegrino allegedly became a nun after her father forced her to break up with her longtime boyfriend, a small-time Baltimore area hood named Swigs McAdams. Most of the time, she studied her new calling quite earnestly, but every now and then she got the urge to secretly visit Swigs and see what he was up to.

It seemed as though every other Saturday between 1953 and 1955, Sister Marie would take a short walk and then discreetly change into a pair of blue jeans and a black sweater before scaling the stone walls of St. Sadie Convent in Baltimore. After spending anywhere from a few hours to several days with Swigs, she would invariably return to St. Sadie's, repent sincerely, and be accepted back into the fold.

Matt: Did she go on these, um, excursions alone?

Hilda: Not always. On some of these clandestine trips, Sister Marie would bring a group of the other nuns with her, comprising a gang that came to be known as either "The Traveling Swigs Sisters," or "Pellegrino's Posse." One of the other ladies, Bertie "Numbers" Culligan, never returned, deciding to pursue a career as a loan shark. Another, Domenica Rosenzsweig, was not accepted back; she received a pink slip to go with her black habit. Domenica became a very successful high school lacrosse coach.

Matt: So what became of "Sweet Feet?"

Hilda: Sister Marie, with her sweet, beatific smile, was accepted back every time, but all the comings and goings had the powers-that-be at St. Sadie's instituting a weekly conventory of their residents.

Eventually, Swigs had a heart-to-heart talk with Marie and convinced her to continue to honor her calling as a nun.

Matt: And what of Swigs?

Hilda: In 1959, fed up with his life in crime and despondent that he could not see Sister Marie anymore, Swigs McAdams went into politics—eventually serving two terms in the Clinton administration.

Cornography

Cornography (n)—explicit images that depict corn in such a way that its primary purpose is to cause sexual arousal

You Know What ... ?

Thomas Shoemilker is a filmmaker of some notoriety. Nicknamed *The King of Cornography,* he has made more than twenty films that critics have ripped apart. Mr. Shoemilker called me from Cedar Rapids, Iowa—the location of his upcoming film, *Stalking the Silk.*

Matt: Mr. Shoemilker, why have so many critics derided your artistic creations?

Thomas: Please call me Shoe. I don't really concern myself with the critics. I've been doing good box office for many years.

Matt: Shoe, let me get right to it. Do you consider your work to be *cornographic?*

Thomas: If you're asking me whether I find corn to be erotic in its natural state, I would say "yes." If you're asking me whether two people making love in a cornfield is alluring and something that moviegoers want to see, I would also say "yes." Does that make my work cornographic? I'll leave that for others to decide.

Matt: Sounds reasonable to me. Have you always had a thing for corn? Did you eat it as a kid? Where did you grow up?

Thomas: A lot of questions there. I've always enjoyed devouring corn on the cob, and I also became a fan of canned corn later in life. In middle school, I was nicknamed "Corndog Tommy" because of all the corn I consumed. I grew up near Corning, Iowa—the birthplace of Johnny Carson.

Matt: How did your love for corn translate into a love for filmmaking and what some might call *cornography*?

Thomas: I fell in love with the films of a diverse crew of great moviemakers like Hitchcock, Capra, Kurosawa, Scorsese and Russ Meyers. During a Russ Meyers film I typically eat two bags of popcorn and four corns on the cob. I guess that I just combined my love for corn, women and cinema to become the self-taught director of a whole cornucopia of classic films.

Matt: Given your obsessive love of corn and your own films with titles such as *Horndog Harry and the Niblet Triplets*, why were you so hard on a fellow filmmaker who released *Stepchildren of the Corn* last year?

Thomas: Listen, Matt. I've been accused of serving up "soft corn" and "hard corn" but nobody has ever accused me of purveying "kiddie corn." I just found the premise of that film to be morally repugnant and not in keeping with the classy images that I bring to the big screen.

Matt: Your most infamous film *Cornfield of Creams* met with great controversy. Any regrets?

Thomas: The critics panned it, but what else is new.

Matt: But the film upon which it was based was a beautiful story of a love for baseball, the pursuit of dreams, second chances at redemption, fathers and sons, and you—

Thomas: I loved *Field of Dreams* as much as you did but you can't deny that it had some highly charged moments of eroticism. The tall fields of corn, the sexy whispers, the messages like "If you build it, he will come," "Ease his pain" and "Go the distance." I just played off all of the latent sexual tension and made it more blatant.

Matt: Maybe so, but was it necessary to have your movie culminate in the father coming back to life and sharing a threes—

Thomas: I'll thank you not to give away the twist ending.

Matt: My bad. We're almost out of time, but I promised to ask you about *Stalking the Silk*.

Thomas: This is a gorgeous, almost elegiac tale of a farm boy's unrequited love for a beautiful tennis player. The tennis player is portrayed very naturalistically by a young actress named Annie Cornokova. There is a breathtaking montage that we just shot of her pounding two–handed backhands through the grass courts of Cedar Rapids. Hauntingly beautiful stuff! And I don't want to tell you too much more about the film but my wife wrote a beautiful song titled *Corn Between Two Lovers*. Would you like to hear a little?

Matt: Well, you've been most generous with your time, and I'd hate to have you—

Thomas: (singing) Corn between two lovers / Playing with the cob / Loving both of you / I feel like such a slob. Corn—

Matt: Thanks, Shoe. Can't wait for the release.

Crapezoid

Crapezoid (n)—an unusual, four-sided toilet in which only two of the sides are parallel to one another

Please Note: In England, there are no crapezoids, but they do have a few **crapeziums**—four-sided toilets with no parallel sides.

You Know What ... ?

Since the crapezoid resembles many old Egyptian structures, there is speculation that this type of toilet originated there. We can neither confirm nor deny that this is true, as so far we have not been able to unearth any such evidence.

What we do know is that one hundred or so years after King Tut died, there lived a pharaoh named King Buttincommon, who would often meet with royal advisors from his very ornate throne. Apparently, Buttincommon used to scribble important legal statutes on special papyrus while relieving himself. If he liked what he wrote, he'd present it to his chief of staff, and if he didn't, he would crumple up the papyrus and flush it. I can relate.

Crustfallen

Crustfallen (adj)—a feeling of dejection caused by a slice of pizza, or the whole pie, falling on the floor

Sample Scenario: Jon and Sandi were enjoying a quiet take-out dinner at home with their daughters, Julie and Mel, when disaster struck. It wasn't *that* disastrous, but you would never know that from the crustfallen expressions on the girls' faces. Their beautiful mushroom and pineapple pizza got knocked over, face down, onto the linoleum. Seeing their crustfallen looks, Sandi immediately called Pogo's Pizza and ordered another two pies.

You Know What ... ?

According to the Falling Fast Food Institute, the five takeout foods most likely to fall to the ground are:

- Pizza (naturally)
- Turkey hoagies
- Fish sandwiches
- Buffalo wings
- Mozzarella sticks

Cryogenitalis

Cryogenitalis (n)—the science of freezing human testicles for long periods of time and observing the sounds emitted by their owners

Please Note: Luckily, this discipline has been discredited from all major universities in the United States, and there has even been great shrinkage in the amount of its informal practitioners.

Sample Scenario: Sally, never a stranger to rotten luck, was excited to move into a luxury Manhattan high-rise apartment building. Unbeknownst to her, her upstairs neighbor was a cryogenitalis fanatic. Never having heard of this science, Sally surmised that Mr. Wicketts was simply a terrible singer.

You Know What ... ?

Dr. Richard Bobosky, of the famed Pullman Institute of Unusual Pleasures, is an expert on the worldwide practice of cryogenitalis. "My research team estimates that 2.3 percent of all adult males have experimented with cryogenitalis at least once. We surveyed 1,012 males who admitted to such experimentation and pulled the following data:

- 0.35 percent recommended this activity to friends
- 65 percent rooted for the Dallas Cowboys
- 81 percent had attended a Tea Party rally, and of that 81 percent, 92 percent stated that they enjoyed cryogenitalis more than the rally

Cubicle Zirconium

Cubicle Zirconium (n)—an artificial diamond worn, ostensibly, to impress coworkers

Observation:

While some people may be able to detect a fake diamond, others (like me) wouldn't know the difference if they studied a CZ under special microscopes for a solid week. I'm also not particularly impressed by the size of rocks, so I'm clearly not the target audience for cubicle zirconium wearers.

Wearing a cubicle zirconium is tricky business. Clearly, the CZ wearer is counting on her coworkers to be impressed yet not knowledgeable enough to spot a fake diamond.

Mastering the Word

When it comes to cubicle zirconiums and real diamonds, are you:

a. able to tell the difference, and it's important?
b. not able to tell the difference, and don't care?
c. not able to tell the difference, but would like to be?
d. able to tell the difference, but don't care?
e. not able to care about this question at all?

Deeplistic

Deeplistic (adj)—characterized by both overly simplistic and very profound analysis, reasoning, or use of emotion

You Know What ... ?

Semanticians (people with little or no lives who debate the *exact* meaning of all words in our lexicon) generally believe that deeplistic does not denote something that is halfway between overly simple and profound—it is both. Edwin Eggnut, president of the American Society of Semanticians Honoring Obligatory Lexicon Exploratory Studies, noted the following about this entry.

"A deeplistic book is one that will both move you with its depth and at the same time shock you with its simplicity. *The Prophet* by Khalil Gibran fits this category for me. By consensus, our society also found the following to be deeplistic: 95 percent of Marc Chagall's paintings; 83 percent of Charlie Kaufman's films; 97 percent of Yogi Berra's observations; and 53 percent of Matthew J. Goldberg's poetry."

When I asked Eggnut why the other 47 percent of my poetry was not considered to be deeplistic, he mentioned that the society had only read 64 percent of it. I ended our discussion 77 percent confused.

Demographiti

Demographiti (n)—Graffiti tailored to a specific audience—i.e., age, ethnic group, income level, or ethnicity

Sample Scenario: Timmy never really enjoyed going with his mom and dad to visit Gramps at his retirement community, but one day his mom was shocked to see him eager to make the monthly trip to Spruce Village. His delighted mom asked him if he enjoyed the checker games with Gramps, to which Timmy replied, "Nah. There's some really cool demographiti on the side of his building I like to look at."

You Know What ... ?

Types of spray-painted demographiti favored most by senior citizens include:

- the names of their grandkids
- their middle names
- their phone numbers
- "Kilroy was here"
- social security numbers
- names of early-bird friendly restaurants

Diaperkinetic

Diaperkinetic (adj)—exhibiting great energy while staining a diaper

Sample Sentence: Having slept little the night before, I prayed that my little Benny would not be able to maintain his diaperkinetic pace.

You Know What ... ?

Dr. Angel Moreno, an expert in diaperkinesiology, has spent years studying the various effects of diaperkinetics on a young baby's metabolism—and vice versa. Moreno states, "In the same way that many school-age children are diagnosed with hyperkinesis, an early pattern of diaperkinesis often shows up as early as two months in age. Many of these babies move uncontrollably, causing their parents to have to change their diapers up to fifteen times daily."

The tough part of all this? "There is no cure for this," notes the good doctor. "The only remedy is patience and lots of coupons to defray some of the cost of all the diapers needed."

Dramadairy

Dramadairy (n)—a morning meal that often includes lots of bagels, cream cheese, butter—and frenetic arguments

Sample Sentence: I told my brother, Brian, that I'd see him around 2:00 PM so as to avoid the family dramadairy.

Observation:

While family strife can erupt no matter what foods are on the menu, there is something about bagels and lox that brings out the dysfunction. (Some of you may disagree with my assertion, and that's one of the beauties of this book. If you disagree, we can verbally duke it out over some bagels and *schmeer*.) So what is that certain something that brings out the drama? I'm not really sure, but it may have something to do with one, or all, of the below:

- the shape of the bagel
- the hole in the middle of it
- the saltiness of the lox (smoked salmon)
- the people at the breakfast table

Earigation

Earigation (n)—the practice of washing one's ears an inordinate amount of times, causing flooding in the alimentary canals

Observation:

My favorite story about earigation is one that I can't certify as factual. But here's how the story goes:

A rather fussy patient named Gareth Watson visited his doctor, Joseph Holmes, to find out why he was having frequent earaches and loss of hearing. Dr. Holmes asked him a few questions and then went on to examine his ears.

As it turned out, there was a surplus of water in Watson's ears, and Holmes asked him if he was careful when bathing. Watson admitted that he washed his ears multiple times every day but had never before encountered this problem. In fact, the patient was quite insistent that there was something else amiss.

Holmes advised him that earigation was the root of the problem, and Watson questioned how he would know that from the brief examination—to which Dr. Holmes famously replied, "It's alimentary, my dear Watson."

Eggxonerate

Eggxonerate (v)—to excuse the person who made you a disgusting breakfast

Sample Scenario: As a youngster, I remember looking forward to my first breakfast at Greg's Greasy Spoon—scrambled eggs, pancakes, and toast. I arrived with my parents and brothers and ended up getting sick. The eggs were runny, the pancakes were burnt, and the toast tasted moldy. When I recovered a couple days later, I vowed to never go back there. My mom pleaded with me to eggxonerate Greg's, and we ended up going back a month later and many more times over the years.

You Know What … ?

The state of New Jersey used to have (maybe it's still on the books) a so-called runny egg law that kept restaurants and diners from serving undercooked (runny) eggs. The result was that many loyal customers ran away from the diners and sopped up their eggs at home. No yoke.

Electrolysister

Electrolysister (n)—a sister or close friend who lends moral support to someone undergoing hair removal

Sample Sentence: Whenever she needed some unwanted hair destroyed, Cheryl traveled to the doctor's office with her trusted electrolysister, Harriet.

Observation:

I spoke to Harriet Fumanchita (see above sample sentence), who said that she would only let her good friend have her hair removed in four different ways:

- laser treatment
- galvanic electrolysis
- thermolytic electrolysis
- a blend of those three methods

When I asked her what she would do if the specialist mentioned that he/she would yank on her friend's unwanted body hair with tweezers until it disappeared, she said something that I would not print in this family edition.

Elephantosis

Elephantosis (n)—a horrific disease caused by exposure to too many Republican politicians

Sample Sentence: After suffering through the Republican National Convention, I woke up the next morning only to find that my legs were swollen and my brain had shrunk—sure signs of elephantosis.

Observation:

My friend Ted Jabberlocky (would I make up that name?) is an ardent Republican who takes issue with this term. Here's part of his rant:

"Elephantosis has never been proven clinically, and besides, what about all of the diseases caused by exposure to too many Democrats? I'd like to call that syndrome *jackassphyxiation*—the lack of focus, out-of-control family spending, and eventual belt tightening brought on by too much exposure to Democrats."

Nice try, Ted. When you get your own book, you can feature that as an entry.

Emroidery

Emroidery (n)—the art of working ornamental designs upon any woven fabric while under the influence of performance-enhancing drugs

You Know What ... ?

Emroidery is a relatively new art form and one with which I was not acquainted until I was introduced to Helga Hummerschmidt, 2009 world champion of backstitch speed emroidery. She consented to a quick interview.

Matt: Helga, congrats on winning the 2009 world championship of speed emroidery. I'll bet all of the German people are quite proud.

Helga: I'm not sure why. I was born and raised in Hamden, Connecticut.

Matt: My mistake. I know nothing about emroidery, but as a humorist, I do also like leaving people in stitches.

Helga: Fascinating.

Matt: Thank you. So tell me, how do steroids and other illegal substances help you in those speed competitions?

Helga: Our competition is anything goes, and the stronger you are, the faster you can get your arms and fingers pumping out creations.

Matt: So how big are those biceps of yours?

Helga: Currently about 16.5 inches. I've eased off some of the juice to compete in appliqué tournaments. Those Victorian-like ladies frown on performance-enhanced competitors, and I'm trying to look daintier.

Matt: Can you describe what your winning emroidery pattern was in last year's competition?

Helga: We had to stitch a pattern of a dragon and at least one other animal into leather. I backstitched a giant dragon strangling a mongoose, and I did it with great intricacy in less than thirty minutes.

Matt: Amazing. I did hear that a lady from Finland, Jaana Faakaalapa, was upset with the decision.

Helga: Yes, the little tramp thought her picture of a dragon feeding a puppy should have won. I laughed in her face and told her to train harder for next year. She called me a backbitch, and I thanked her for the compliment. This is not your grandmother's competition anymore. We stitch for keeps.

Eurologist

Eurologist (n)—one who studies foreign currency, especially but not exclusively those of the twelve European Union Nations

Sample Sentence: When I gave Tina an Israeli shekel, she studied it so thoroughly that I thought she was giving it a eurological exam.

Please Note: It used to be that Israeli coin fetishists like Tina would be called "Shekelologists," but the term soon lost its status when their main networking group, Shekelologists Holding Industry Training, folded and became a part of Eurological Anal Technicians.

Observation:

A rousing good time for many eurologists is a pot-luck dinar dinner party where pizza is always served but the guests may bring dinars from all the countries where it is used. Eligible currency may come from countries such as Algeria, Bahrain, Iraq, Libya, and Tunisia. These are spirited parties, but be careful: many a guest has been known to have been thrown out for unwittingly bringing in a Moroccan dirham.

Fairinheight

Fairinheight (adj)—euphemism for short in stature

Fairinheight (n)—euphemism for a person who is short in stature

Sample Sentence: Ally thought that her neighbor, Chazz, would've been hot if he weren't so fairinheight.

You Know What ... ?

There is a strong belief that taller people (especially taller men) have an advantage over their shorter counterparts in most competitive pursuits, including sports, scoring chicks, job promotions, and presidential campaigns. While there may be some truth to this old canard, I studied our past presidential elections to see how often the "fairinheight" candidate defeated his taller opponent.

My review produced some interesting results:
- In competitive elections, where the heights of both or all candidates were known (and there wasn't a tie), the taller man won twenty-four times and lost nineteen. The fairinheights did better than I would have expected.
- One recent president who defeated taller men was George Bush II (listed at 6' even, he defeated the 6'4" John Kerry and the 6'1" Al Gore.) Perhaps his lower IQ was a compensating factor.
- One giant killer was James Madison (the shortest prez, at 5'4") who yielded eleven inches to De Witt Clinton and still chopped him down to size. Another similarly impressive performance was 5'10" Franklin Pierce's 1852 defeat of the 6'5" Winfield "Old Fuss and Feathers" Scott.
- A successful giant was Abe Lincoln (6'4"), who used his height advantage to crush his opponents, including George

McClellan (5'8") and Stephen Douglas, a (Madisonian 5'4").

My All-Presidential Basketball Team:

Point Guard—James "Half-Pint" Madison

Shooting Guard—Barack Obama: 6'4", long arms, and still a decent shooter (some would say he moves well, if not exclusively, to his left)

Small Forward—Thomas (TJ) Jefferson: 6'2"-plus, and brilliant

Power Forward—LBJ: 6'4"-plus, with a nasty attitude

Center—**Abraham** (A-Train) Lincoln: who else?

Fakethrough

Fakethrough (n)—a very trivial discovery or artificial watershed moment

You Know What ... ?

Below is a list of five great scientific inventions (breakthroughs) of the twentieth century, contrasted with **some corresponding fakethroughs of dubious significance.**

1903—Orville Wright (cheered on by Wilbur) manned the first powered air flight.
1906—Peter Steckel (egged on by classmate Becky Manson) flew the first paper airplane to hit history teacher Babette Connors in the nose.

1924—Clarence Birdseye was credited with starting us on the road to frozen food.
1976—George "Birdbrain" Blaustein ate twelve pounds of uncooked, frozen succotash to win $24.

1926— Robert Goddard invented the liquid fuel rocket.
1993—Bill "Rocket" Sinclair downed a quart of lighter fluid before successfully parachuting off a plane in Hohokus, New Jersey.

1944—Willem Kolff invented the kidney dialysis machine.
1943—William Cough patented a knife that is able to cut kidney beans in half without losing their nutrients.

1951—Carl Djerassi invented the oral contraceptive pill.
1952—Carol Djerassi (still) just said, "No."

Fartissimo

Fartissimo (adv)—very loudly—as in music that is played so forcefully that it causes the musician or orchestra leader to break wind

Sample Sentence: With my bowels already churning, I prayed that my oboe would make enough noise to muffle my own gas when I played the fartissimo section of Wagner's Die Meistersinger.

You Know What ... ?

The late, great Sashayuri Breakowsky was maestro of the Moscow Philharmonic from 1948 till his abrupt death in 1998. Breakowsky died while conducting a most spirited performance of Rachmaninoff's Piano Concerto Number 2. Oddly enough, Breakowsky had steadfastly refused to have his orchestra play certain pieces by Rachmaninoff and Shostakovich because they called for lots of fartissimo. Breakowsky famously was quoted below.

"There is a lot of great music out there, without having to play these risky compositions. Let's say we perform Shostakovich and there is very little ventilation in the room, and then one of our bassoon players had eaten a little too much before the performance. It's just not worth turning our philharmonic into a wind ensemble—don't you think?"

Breakowsky spoke great wisdom, although ironically (or was it fittingly?) he was done in by Number 2.

Feastiality

Feastiality (n)—sexual relations with a plate of food

Warning:

This is a difficult one to write about, and you'll thank me for not painting too many word pictures here. *Feastiality* is most often used in the figurative sense, not the literal.

Sample Sentence: Alfredo enjoyed his seafood platter so thoroughly that many people in the restaurant thought that he was engaging in feastiality.

You Know What ... ?

Rhonda Sweetknee, of the Center For American Sexual and Food Disorders, identified these five foods as inspiring the most cases of feastiality:

- Lobster thermidor
- Rosemary chicken
- Knockwurst
- Quiche Lorraine
- Anything by *Mrs. Paul*

Fictionary

Fictionary (adj)—descriptive of a dreamed about but unrealized sexual position where the man lies on top of his partner

Please Note: Fictionary is derived from the roots for fiction and missionary. It has nothing to do with any compendium of falsified words.

Sample Sentence: Jonesy is always regaling us with his exploits, most of which reek of the fictionary position.

You Know What ... ?

A scan of various polls shows that about 60 percent of high school boys and 30 percent of high school girls claim to have had sexual intercourse at least once. This would seem to indicate that at least one of the following statements is true:

a. the active girls are twice as active as the boys
b. the *active* boys engage in twice as much fictionary as the girls.

Fidouchiary

Fidouchiary (adj)—of or pertaining to the relationship between a woman and her special cleansing apparatus

Observation:

While the first four letters spell "Fido," this has nothing to do with dogs. It also has nothing to do with the FDIC—founded in 1933 to ensure the safety of bank deposits. That is unless the FDIC stood for Feminine ... oh, never mind.

Sample Scenario: Tilda Summerstock hated cleaning her house and loathed balancing the budget. But to her everlasting credit, she took her fidouchiary responsibilities seriously and was known as the cleanest girl in town.

The Fifth Beetle

The Fifth Beetle (n)—the beetle that comes into view after you have already spotted four and before you have spotted the sixth one. What, you were expecting me to mention Pete Best?

You Know What ... ?

Obviously, John, Paul, George, and Ringo are the four most famous Beatles—the world's greatest rock and roll band of all time. But what about the lowly beetle?

The beetle (yeah, yeah, yeah) is said to have more species than any other living creature. My own personal "Mount Rushmore" of beetles would have to include:

- The rhinoceros beetle—a fierce bastard that flies around with a horn on its head and can lift up to 850 times its own weight
- The Japanese beetle—super fast and also bilingual
- The bombardier beetle—soars through the air shooting deadly sprays
- *Beetle Bailey*—a comic strip created by Mort Walker about a lazy Army private
- The Fifth Beetle—do we really need one?

FlatuLENT

FlatuLENT (adj)—exhibiting no excess accumulation of gas and trying hard not to break wind during the forty days from Ash Wednesday to Easter

Sample Sentence: While a reliable breaker of wind during the other 325 days of the calendar year, Susie was, ironically, quite flatuLENT during the holy days.

Observation:

This word, itself, is somewhat ironical, as capitalizing L-E-N-T at the end of the word gives it a whole new meaning.

The idea of observing a flatuLENT period is very controversial and consequently is not practiced by many churches. As my friend, the very compassionate Father Michael Patrick Sean Muldoon-Rosenberg, explained to me, "I'm all for less gas during the holy days, but the members of my church are already foregoing many other activities and vices during this time. It would be unfair to put them under further gastric duress, and take their mind off of their prayer."

Fore-iron or Fore-wood

Fore-iron or Fore-wood (n)—a golf shot hit so poorly that that you fear that it is about to strike some poor schmuck on the head

Please Note: Duffer McPurdy, my golf consultant and friend, informs me that before the term *fore-iron* was chosen, several other names were proposed—including *look-out-wood, oh-crap-iron,* and *##@@!-wedge.*

You Know What ... ?

Golf is hardly considered a very physical sport, but millions of avid golfers suffer lower back, neck, and wrist injuries every year. And what about all of the injuries caused by errant fore-irons?

There are two things that especially irk me on the golf course, besides my own poor play. One is the lack of half-decent food and drink in the clubhouse. The other is the lack of warning when an errant shot is headed for my noggin from the club of an impatient jerk from another party.

Some good news: Golf ball manufacturers are said to be working on a special ball that will yell "duck" whenever it flies within ten feet of a human being or cuddly pet. Be on the lookout for it.

Freudian Slipcover

Freudian Slipcover (n)—a fitted protective cover for fancy upholstered furniture—used mostly by psychiatrists

You Know What ... ?

Dr. Klaus Stichmein is the owner of the Klaus House of Furniture and Psychoanalysis, a thriving business in his native St. Louis, Missouri. I was able to book a free twenty-five-minute phone conversation with Klaus, which is partially recorded below.

Matt: Doctor, can you tell me more about the origin of Freudian slipcovers?

Klaus: Why not! Sigmund Freud, the great and controversial father of modern psychiatry and psychoanalysis, was the father of the slipcover as well. He used to encourage his patients to consult with him in a very relaxed atmosphere, but the furniture he used was very formal and expensive. Ever the genial host, he used to serve his patients drinks, but many of those drinks would be spilled—especially when the patient inspired an "aha moment."

Matt: So why didn't Freud stop serving them drinks?

Klaus: Dr. Freud once famously wrote, "Serving my patients drinks stimulates new channels of communication, even freeing up layers of the unconscious. It also helps to kill time during our sessions, and is a wonderful way to encourage follow-up explorations." Freud was also a brilliant businessman, and he asked a tailor who was a patient (and sometimes referred to as Tailor B) to make him some slipcovers in exchange for reduced-fee sessions. There was no microfiber back then.

Matt: So tell me about these "aha moments."

Klaus: An "aha moment" would come about during sessions of psychoanalysis, often when the patient was drinking a cup of coffee and free associating about something. One notable example of this came when Patient XX, who had an aversion to eating wiener schnitzel, was chit-chatting with Freud in a calm way about his dog, Fritzi. When he casually mentioned that he once saw Fritzi eat a wiener schnitzel with sauerkraut, the normally mild-mannered Freud abruptly exclaimed, "Aha!" This caused Patient XX to splatter the couch he was sitting on, as well as Dr. Freud, with hot java.

Matt: So where was the "aha" in that?

Klaus: The good doctor correctly surmised that his patient felt that if he ate wiener schnitzel, especially if served with sauerkraut, he would become a sexual predator to all the librarians in Vienna.

Matt: Astonishing. So tell me, Klaus, do Freudian slipcovers have anything to do with Freudian slips?

Klaus: You are referring, of course, to the slips of our tongues known as parapraxes, as in when you are having sex with your wife and scream out the name of a former girlfriend?

Matt: Um, yeah, those.

Klaus: No, it has nothing to do with that. It's all about protecting furniture.

Matt: I think I see. So as an astute businessman, how do you combine selling furniture and counseling?

Klaus: The two really go hand in hand. As a furniture salesman, I get to the bottom of what fabric a customer really desires, and as an analyst, I can recommend the furniture and slipcover that best frees up my clients' subconscious. More practically, we also run some great promotions here. This week only, with the purchase of any ottoman, all new customers are entitled to an introductory session at 50 percent off. One of my favorite promos yet!

Frogmentation

Frogmentation (n)—the act of cutting a frog into sections, either for biological research or just for the heck of it

Observation:

Show of hands: how many of you had to perform a frogmentation in junior high or high school biology class? Oddly enough, while other kids were putting frogs and fetal pigs in their lockers, I never got the chance to take anything apart other than an earthworm. No, I didn't take the short bus to school, and yes (amazingly enough), I was generally an A student. I just never had a very rigorous or interesting science class. Just thought I'd share. Hands down, please; we don't know where they've been!

You Know What ... ?

The National Frogmentation Institute estimates that the four most commonly dissected animals in American high schools are:

1. Frogs
2. Dogfish sharks
3. Lab (and gym) rats
4. Cafeteria mystery meat

Frustracean

Frustracean (n)—the feeling of anxiety and despair caused by an inability to crack open a shellfish

Please Note: For those who keep kosher, it describes the feelings of insecurity and inferiority caused by not being allowed to eat lobster.

Observation:

Interestingly enough, only lobster (not shrimp or crabs) inspires frustracean among those committed to keeping kosher.

Sample Scenario: Kristen was enjoying her favorite dinner at Sammy's Seafood, savoring every inch of her Maine lobster drenched with butter. While usually a quite considerate person, she was oblivious to what was happening to her cross-the-table dinner mate. Sitting with the two of them, I watched Chaim's mounting frustracean as he trudged through his piece of baked codfish.

Gastrophysicist

Gastrophysicist (n)—a scientist who explores the effects of interplanetary travel on the human digestive system

Observation:

Gastrophysics is a new field, and as such, is only taught at nineteen colleges and universities in the United States—only four of which field competitive Division 1-A football teams.

Mastering the Word

Which of the following would be something a gastrophysicist *might* be concerned with?

- How quickly a tuna hoagie is devoured by a former astronaut
- How many onions a Martian can eat at a single sitting
- The price of pasta primavera on Neptune
- How much a gallon of gas costs
- All of the above
- Next page, please!

Gondoliery

Gondoliery or gondoleery (adj)—pertaining to the wariness of being taken for a ride by someone who mans a gondola

Sample Scenario: Carol was having a great time on her first trip to Venice with her husband, Paul. When he suggested that they take a romantic ride in one of the famed gondolas, Carol saw its sleazy-looking operator and got very gondoliery.

You Know What ... ?

Jamal Ponatella, President of Keepin' it Real Vacations, told me, "Everyone wants to go to Venice and see the beauty of the so-called Queen of the Adriatic. That's okay. But we suggest that you (if you must go) avoid the gondolas. A short ride will set you back about a hundred euros, and once you're in the boat, the gondolier will sing a verse of "That's Amore," and expect an extra fifty."

Jamal's advice? "Take the stinking speedboats, man. You'll spend half as much, see everything faster, and not have to hear any cheesy singing."

Grossery

Grossery (n)—a disgusting item sold in a supermarket or in a market specializing in the sale of such items

Sample Sentence: Betty examined her grossery list, which included olive loaf, pickled beets, and lima beans.

Please Note: Grossery is highly subjective; one man's grossery is another man's delicacy.

You Know What ... ?

The top eight grossery items of 2009, as identified by *Savvy Shopping Philadelphia* readers, were:

- Olive loaf
- Turnips
- Brussels sprouts
- Moldy cheese—still no match for the top three
- Molasses
- Lima beans
- Prune juice
- Indian candy corn

Gruntled

Gruntled (adj)—in a state halfway between somewhat pleased and greatly dissatisfied

Sample Sentence: While I would not totally pan the new overpriced fusion restaurant, the so-so food left me feeling a bit gruntled.

You Know What ... ?

For the latest on this new wordapod, I sat down with historian and semantician supreme Edwin Eggnut.

Matt: Hey Eddie, are you feeling gruntled today?

Eggnut: No, but glad you asked. Not really. My lunch left me a little disturbed, but on the whole, I'm quite pleased with my day.

Matt: I think my readers will be quite pleased to know that. So what can you tell me about the word *gruntled*?

Eggnut: The term was coined in 1953 by an obscure union leader named Cesar Goldstein—head of the Latino Jewish Farm Workers Association (LJFWA). Goldstein felt that too much attention was paid to happy employees on the one hand and to the disgruntled, ready-to-strike employees on the other. As Cesar famously said in a speech before five dozen or so diehard supporters, "I come before you today to recognize that management is turning a blind eye to your needs. Are they giving you all the tools you need to perform at greatest efficiency? *No.* Are they taking care of you and your family's needs? *No.* Are we going to strike? *No*—not yet! Are you guys happy? *No.* Are you disgruntled? *No*—not really. We are the silent majority! *We are the gruntled!* And we demand that management listen to us as well!

Matt: Simply mesmerizing. Did you memorize all that?

Eggnut: *No!* Just kidding. Actually, as a kid, my dad encouraged me to memorize a lot of famous speeches.

Matt: So what happened to this association, and why had I never heard of them before?

Eggnut: Cesar Goldstein, a most generous man, invited all of his supporters out for lunch after the rally. The mob couldn't decide on where to eat and started to argue. Goldstein was unable to control them and threw his hands up in despair. By the time he was about to suggest Chinese food as a compromise, lunch was ruined, and they never recovered their momentum.

Matt: That's a shame. What happened to Goldstein?

Eggnut: He tried to rally another group of migrant workers, but they turned instead to more radical voices. Still, not totally dissatisfied with his idea, in 1990 he founded the Association of Gruntled Retired Energy Employees, known as AGREE.

Matt: I've never heard of them. Sounds like yet another failure.

Eggnut: The 553 members of AGREE might beg to differ—in a polite fashion, of course.

Guesstaurant

Guesstaurant (n)—where one goes for pot-luck dinners

Sample Sentence: Milly pleaded with Herbie to tell her of their dinner plans, but he insisted on taking her to his favorite guesstaurant.

Observation:

Even if one tends to go to the same restaurant every time, it's still considered a *guesstaurant* if the venue isn't announced ahead of time.

According to the editors of *Mediocre Dining Illustrated*, the top methods used to come up with the right guesstaurant include:

- Dartboards
- Ouija boards
- *Being* bored (and just driving or walking)
- Blindfolds
- Coin flipping
- The Magic 8-Ball
- Benoit Balls (if desperate enough)

Gulagarithm

Gulagarithm (n)—a mathematical or other scientific theorem written from the confines of a prison camp

Sample Sentence: When the Soviet officials imprisoned Sergei, they did not envision all of the gulagarithms the brilliant mathematician would create.

You Know What ... ?

Many of the great mathematical theorems in history have been postulated by men and women while incarcerated. Two very profound ones are listed below.

In 1968, Alexei Rubanov, while in Siberia, gave us the famous Frozen Rope Theorem, which (in so many words) said: "If two knots on a string laid out on a tangential plane along contiguous axes are dipped in water and left outside at -10 degrees Celsius or lower, the distance between those knots will lessen in proportion to the amount the rope shrinks by freezing."

One hundred or so years prior to Rubanov, George Nathans, a Union soldier, wrote the Theorem of Assimilated Colors from his cell at the confederate prison in Salisbury, North Carolina. His groundbreaking ToAC Theorem stated unambiguously, "If a bluish color within the visible spectrum producing light within a wavelength between 450 and 500 nm is overrun by a dull color between the hues of black and white (and considered to be grey), the following physical phenomena may be apparent:

- the blue will be subsumed by the grey as if captured on a battlefield
- the essential characteristics of the blue will be assimilated over time and refracted indefinitely until fragments of green

and violet appear prior to its disintegration and re-entry after seventeen reincarnations."

Nathans' theorem has many parts, the last of which is less theoretical and very practical, (which I'll paraphrase): "If articles of blue and grey are mixed with a blood-red (an extreme color at the end of the visible spectrum with a wavelength between 610 and 780 nm), special care should be taken not to wash them in the same load unless the water utilized is less than 58 degrees Fahrenheit."

With such wisdom available to us, we can only wonder what other theorems they would have given us had they been free men.

Haikugar

Haikugar (n)—a woman who is aggressively into younger men who recite haiku

Observation:

The term *cougar* is a fairly recent one coined to describe a woman who preys on younger men. This fact has me wondering:

    a. Why a cougar and not a mountain lion, catamount, or puma?

    b. Is this term pejorative for women? If not, then what is the male counterpart called?

You Know What ... ?

Lisa Primstuffel started a club in her native Honolulu called Hawaiian Haikugars on the Prowl. As she explains, "I see nothing derisive about the term. We are a group of refined ladies who know what we want—twenty-something boys or the right thirty-something men to read us seventeen-syllable romantic poetry while we wine and dine them. Is there something wrong with that?"

> ***What can be better***
> ***Haikugars on the rampage***
> ***Oh no, I'm married.***

Halloweiner

Halloweiner (n)—a hot dog—usually a cocktail frank or piece of sausage—given out to trick-or-treaters

You Know What ... ?

The custom of giving out Halloweiners is so widespread in certain parts of Indiana that many young kids bring mustard, ketchup, and relish packets with them when strolling around the neighborhood.

The tradition apparently began when Lorraine Wilson, a kindly lady from Kokomo, wanted to give the "lovely children from the neighborhood" something with a little more nutritional value. An octogenarian with a den mother's sensibilities, Lorraine would often give them turkey or vegetable Halloweiners. She would ask them to bring their own condiments and caution them to chew their food slowly without their masks on.

Sample Sentence: Being a vegetarian, Patrick gave a Halloweiner to his friend Madison in exchange for her box of candy. (Not a bad deal, by the way.)

Highway Slobbery

Highway Slobbery (n)—the phenomenon of a large dog covering you with salivary juices as you're driving down the road

Alternatively, *highway slobbery* can describe a sloppy kiss from your most annoying relative when you're stuck in the car with him/her.

Sample Sentence: Mr. Chu complained, "I love to take to the road with my Rottweiler, Jake, but all that highway slobbery is killing me."

Observation:

Everyone must have an "Aunt Edna" or "Uncle Ned" (names chosen at random) who find you irresistible and need to pinch your cheeks or plant a wet one on your cheeks or lips when you're just trying to enjoy the car ride. Perhaps, because of these early childhood formative experiences, you now associate all kisses with the mothballs from Ned's preserved jacket, or maybe it's the interesting perfume that Edna is wearing that lodges in your memory.

Whatever the exact details, everyone has had this experience. Haven't you?

Hit-and-Shun

Hit-and-shun (adj)—a type of traffic accident between Amish buggies that causes both of the (often inebriated) parties to be shunned from the community

You Know What ... ?

Obadiah Stoltzfus is the unofficial town historian for the small, vibrant Amish community of Ephrata, PA. I spoke to him about an infamous hit-and-shun incident from 1983 that is still reverberating around his community.

Matt: Am I correct, Mr. Stoltzfus, that there was a particularly memorable buggy accident between two teenagers in the summer of '83?

Obadiah: That's the truth. I am sure that you are referring to that little dustup between Jeremiah Herr and Jakob Goodfellow.

Matt: Yes, that's the one. Can you tell us about it?

Obadiah: Well, Jakob and Jeremiah were good, earnest young men. They were also a little too high-spirited for most of the elders' tastes. And they often liked to drink some of that old potato moonshine. One hot August day, they were leaving church and started down the dirt road toward Intercourse That's a real town, you know. Have you been there?

Matt: Not often, but I've heard it's beautiful. So they were going down—

Obadiah: Yes. Well, I think they were both trying to impress young Hannah Groutmeyer—

Matt: Were they getting "buggy" with it?

Obadiah: Not sure what you're driving at there. So they got their buggies cranked up, the horses got frightened, and before you knew it, the two boys suffered lacerations.

Matt: That's terrible. What happened to the boys?

Obadiah: The elders got wind of it, and we never saw hide nor hair of Jakob and Jeremiah again.

Matt: And what about the horses and the buggies?

Obadiah: Well, the buggies were brought into Samuel's, and he fixed them up real good, but the poor horses were never able to attend church again.

Hungarees

Hungarees (n)—a pair of pants, usually made of blue denim, that cause the wearer to become very hungry

Sample Sentence: After returning home from dinner quite bloated, Ursula ordered me to take off my hungarees—which she promptly burned.

You Know What ... ?

The first pair of hungarees was sold by a company in San Modesto, California, called the Dungaree Outlet and Diner. Its former owner, Jules Snowcraft, told us all about his brainstorm.

"I had a designer friend who was raving about a pair of pants he made that caused him to overeat every time he wore them. I thought he was crazy, but every time I wore them, they had the very same effect on me, and I'm not a huge eater with normal trousers on. Still a little skeptical, I experimented with these pants over the course of six more months, and as God is my witness, I continued to eat like a Viking each and every time.

"My friend and I patented these pants as Smiley Slacks—admittedly not a brilliant name—and I bought the diner next door to my clothing outlet. We would allow our customers to try their clothes on for up to two hours, and many would walk right next door to the diner. Well, it did wonders for business!"

When asked what it was about the Smiley Slacks that made them such effective hungarees, Snowcraft was still puzzled. "Matt, I wish I knew, but my designer put something in the denim that just caused people's appetites to expand. And the beauty of it was that the jeans would still fit afterwards and look good as well."

So what became of these pants, and the diner for that matter? "We were in California, and for whatever reason, people there just don't get off on eating like barnyard animals. I was going to either move east or try to sell the business, but we encountered three problems:

- My wife didn't want to move
- The food at my diner was pretty lousy
- The color of the hungarees faded after a few months."

I guess that old hackneyed saying is true. Old hungarees never die; they just fade away.

Imashination

Imashination (n)—the special ability to use potatoes creatively

You Know What ... ?

The greatest known use of imashination was exhibited by an otherwise little known minor league catcher named Dave Bresnahan. With special thanks to www.baseballreliquary.org, here is a quick, paraphrased account of Bresnahan's great potato trick:

In August of 1987, Bresnahan, then a twenty-five-year-old backup catcher with the Williamsport (Pennsylvania) Bills of the Class-AA Eastern League, used great imashination during an otherwise meaningless, late-season game.

Prior to the game, Bresnahan skillfully peeled and sculpted a potato in the shape of a baseball. Behind the plate in the fifth inning, with the potato concealed in his mitt and a runner on third base, he purposely threw the potato over his third baseman's head, hoping that the runner would think he made an errant pickoff throw. The play worked to perfection! The runner at third trotted home, where Bresnahan tagged him out with the (real) baseball.

An umpire later retrieved the potato and awarded the runner home because of the catcher's deception.

The following day, Bresnahan was fined by his manager and later released by the Bills' parent club, the Cleveland Indians, for what they considered to be an affront to the integrity of the game.

My suspicion is that if someone like Bill Veeck (a legendary, eccentric owner with the St. Louis Browns, Cleveland Indians, and Chicago White Sox) ran the team, Bresnahan would not have been released—he may have even been promoted and given a raise for this brilliant feat.

But some baseball teams have no imashination whatsoever. Call them "spuddy-duddy!"

Informaldehyde

Informaldehyde (n)—a colorless, toxic compound prepared casually in laboratories and used for the following purposes:

- as a permanent adhesive for certain flooring
- as finishes for certain textiles
- as part of a testing agent for chemists
- as a wash for certain photographic procedures
- as a disinfectant to kill bacteria and fungi
- as an embalming solution

You Know What ... ?

With so many important and sometimes deadly applications, informaldehyde has become quite controversial. In fact, informaldehyde has been outlawed in many countries for any or all of the following reasons:

- It can be used as a biocide
- The preparation process is too casual and leads to many false embalmings—quite embarrassing
- It flies in the face of the convention that bodies should be embalmed in more formal attire.

Inrageous

Inrageous (adj)—so sensible that it offends a more normal person's sensibilities

Observation:

In my experience, most people are just a little irrational, but most of us know at least one person who is always level-headed, rational, and just a little bit too reasonable.

Sample Scenario:

Molly was always trying to convince her husband, Hans, to be just a little more spontaneous. When they went on vacation, Hans planned the itincraries, almost down to the minute. (He did build in fifteen minutes of free time per day for bathroom and water breaks, but you get the idea.)

On their fifth day of touring Italy, Molly noticed a nice gelato stand, but Hans dissuaded her, telling her that: a) they didn't have time to stop and still walk briskly to their awaiting gondola; b) it was an expense that was not budgeted for; and c) she would regret the extra calories it contained.

Molly listened to his inrageous appeal and then calmly walked over to the stand. She returned with a nice amarena gelato, took one bite, and then smashed the rest of it in Hans's face.

There's a lesson in there somewhere.

Jewbilation

Jewbilation (n)—a Jewish celebration—such as a bar or bat mitzvah, confirmation, or wedding

Sample Sentence: Hoping for the ultimate Jewbilation, Marcus Spurling invested $125,000 in his son Dustin's bar mitzvah.

Observation:

Back in my day, bar mitzvah parties were not the big business and high-society event that they have become. Both of my older brothers and I studied our butts off for our respective bar mitzvah services and then celebrated with a nice little gathering at our house. As I recall, my childhood friend and neighbor, Jeff Greenberg, did do the ornate country club celebration—with caviar and all the works—but that was the exception back then.

Enter Myra Grossbeck, founder and owner of Jersey Jewbilations since 1947. "Oy, can I tell you stories? Used to be a time when we would just set up a nice three- to four-hour affair in our main catering hall. Did you see it? It's newly refurbished, and immaculate. *Immaculate!*

"Then, about the 1970s, everyone had to have the ultimate party. And we were right there on the cutting edge. For the next twenty years, if you knew your boy or girl was going to be raised Jewish, you needed to book with us before their bris, or you'd be shut out. *Shut out!*"

I asked Myra if that's changed in the current economy. "Very good question, mister. We're still doing a brisk business because we're the Jewbilation experts. *Experts!*" (I asked her again.)

"No, not really. Just give me a month's notice and I'll make you the party of your dreams—one that will have all your neighbors, relatives, and business colleagues jealous. *Jealous!* I do it all. The seating, the staging, and I arrange for the greatest entertainers in all of the Delaware Valley."

Valley!

Joggles

Joggles (n)—protective eyewear favored by those walking or running at low speeds

Sample Sentence: I didn't feel right during my three-mile job around town, and then I discovered that I left my joggles at home and was wearing my safety goggles instead.

You Know What ... ?

In a poll conducted by *Slow Runners Personnified*, readers responded to the question, "Why do you wear joggles?" Some of the replies were:

- They protect me from stones and dirt kicked up at low speeds.
- They discourage dogs from scratching and biting me.
- They're cool and high-tech looking.
- They provide the right mixture of safety and fashion.
- They give the impression that I'm jogging faster than I truly am.
- They keep me focused on the road ahead.

Knocker Spaniel

Knocker Spaniel (n—pejorative)—a woman with a homely face but appealing chest

Please Note: Apparently, canine breeders once produced a breed of dog that was distinguished by its silky coat, long droopy ears, and buxom chest. Not sure if any still exist.

Sample Sentence: While Judy was no beauty queen, my friends were jealous of me for dating such a loyal knocker spaniel.

You Know What ... ?

No, the author of this book is not sexist; he's just an out-of-control **punndit** (please see entry). Which is worse?

Knocker Spaniel is a younger relative of the infamous "butterface," as in "everything but-her-face looked good." Having said that, I've never used the *butterface* expression, and indeed, a knocker spaniel has other standards to meet.

What would the male equivalent be? An *Ab-ghan*? *Peckinese*? Miniature something? Nah—just a dog!

Lactatorship

Lactatorship (n)—a repressive form of government in which the ruling class forces everyone to drink milk

Observation:

I have often wondered if a lactatorship could happen today, with all of the lactose-intolerant people around. I usually hypothesize that it easily could take place, as alas, it would be a lactatorship and not a democracy. After speaking to my friend, the historian of the unusual, Lars Rottwalico, I may reconsider. As Lars reminded me, "You may recall that one of the Punjabi states in India experimented with a lactatorship in the early twentieth century." (I'd never heard of it— must be slipping.)

"Militant milk and yogurt magnate Raja Gupta Mirza seized power and demanded that all of his subjects drink at least two gallons of milk each day. At his coronation ceremony, millions of lactose-intolerant protesters chugged tall glasses of milk in unison. Fifteen or so minutes later, hundreds of thousands of these protesters were gurgling, belching, and heaving, making a mockery of Mr. Mirza's speech. Mirza abandoned the policy within a week, and the great Punjabi lactatorship was soon abolished as well."

Launduress

Launduress (n—archaic)—a washerwoman who launders and irons clothes under extreme hardship

Sample Sentence: My wife screamed at me that my slovenly ways and demanding nature conspired to make her feel like a launduress.

You Know What ... ?

While *launduress* is an archaic word, two new derivatives of this word are under consideration for our next edition. They are:

- **Lawnduress (n)**—the stress and hardship placed on a person while mowing the lawn. This is an important term describing the pressure put on otherwise normal people by their lawn-obsessed neighbors.

- **Laundude (n)**—a man who is forced by circumstance to do all of his own laundering and ironing

- **Lawndude (n)**—a man who is forced by circumstance to do all of his own yard work

Lavatorium

Lavatorium (n)—a large bathroom equipped with a soundstage and rows of seats—most often utilized by rich, eccentric exhibitionists

Sample Sentence: While I thoroughly enjoyed my visit to Mr. Highmore's estate, I could have done without the sights, sounds, and smells emanating from his lavatorium.

You Know What ... ?

Below is an excerpt taken from a phone interview I conducted with Duncan Roberson, author of the popular coffee-table classic, *Luscious Lavatoriums.*

Matt: Mr. Roberson, I enjoyed your book, and until I get a coffee table, I will display it prominently in my own bathroom.

Duncan: Thank you, but please call me Duncan, or Dunk.

Matt: Dunk, can you tell about any of the eccentric lavatorium owners in your book?

Duncan: Absolutely. My own favorite was a Hollywood producer named Laszlo Schmidt. Schmidt was already a wealthy man in his native Hungary before coming to LA and building a spectacular estate called Schmidtland.

Matt: How did he amass his fortune in Hungary?

Duncan: That's not relevant, Matt. As I was saying, he had a spectacular estate called Schmidtland. He used to host grand parties there with all the muckety-mucks in Hollywood—Gable, Lombard, the whole schmeer. On the tours of his mansion, the showstopper would be his lavatorium. He even called it the "tenth wonder of the world." The bathroom was amazing. It was said to have seating for twelve hundred people and a sound system so ahead of its time that you could hear Chaplin and Keaton speaking.

Matt: What about the bathroom sounds?

Duncan: Every tinkle, sprinkle, plop, and drop was conveyed beautifully to all who were seated in the lavatorium. Should I tell your readers about the time Fatty Arbuckle visited and dropped by Schmidt's throne?

Matt: Nah. Sounds *too* relevant. Thank you for dropping some knowledge on us.

Lefties

Lefties (n)—slang for anything leftover—typically the remnants from a meal that are worth keeping

Sample Sentence: Luigi loved his mom's mammoth Sunday dinners, which always provided substantial lefties for Monday and Tuesday.

Observation:

Last year, my wife and I conferred on a new menu/diet that would help me lose a few pounds. Much to my chagrin, dessert barely made an appearance. Breakfasts featured bagels, cereal, pancakes, fruit, and eggs. Dinners had more variety, mostly featuring fish, vegetables, salad, lentil soup, and chicken, with only a modicum of red meat.

What about lunch? Lots and lots of lefties!

True story. Maybe not riveting, but "true story."

REVIEW Of FIRST 101

Your mission is to fill in the blanks in this story with any of the new wordapods from the preceding pages. Get it? (Got it.) Good.

Jason would be considered by most to be a nice guy, but he was also a single guy who felt a need for female companionship, and he was not the type to pay for it. One evening he took a colleague out to dinner, but she enjoyed her food a little too much for his liking. Jason suspected that she was into _____. They decided to become friends, and she planned to attend his next concert, where he would proudly play his _____ while she would refrain from eating too noticeably.

So where would he find his next girlfriend? Jason pondered this as he sipped at his horrible cup of _____. (Although ravenous, as he was wearing his _____, he wasn't hungry enough to enjoy *that* concoction.) None of his African American friends invited him over for a _____ _____ _____, and he didn't want to go to a poetry reading, where there were likely to be some _____(s) in attendance.

Jason studied his shopping list, acknowledging that he would try to meet some ladies at the meat market. He left his house for the market, also bringing his _____ list just in case. What else would he need? Well, he reasoned, he could discreetly scout women in the distant aisles, so he also brought along a pair of _____(s).

In the produce aisle, Jason spotted a biker-babe-type, who was wearing a _____. Trying to impress her, he started to juggle some potatoes. "That takes *some* _____," Donna said with a smile. Jason started to talk to her but found out that they had very little in common. They didn't even like the same foods; Jason preferred fish, and Donna was something of a _____. They wished each other well, and Jason even offered her to take her out for a nice, refreshing _____ at the custard stand.

Jason pushed his cart down the aisles, pretending to fill up the basket, but there were very few ladies in the market. Oh, he did almost hurt his neck when he _____ to see a five- hundred-pound man, but that was not why he came. Resigned to packing it in for the day, Jason made one more loop around the store. From a distance, he spotted a woman with a beautiful body in aisle fifteen. Was this the break he needed, or was it simply a _____ of sorts?

Jason, no Brad Pitt himself, wheeled over to aisle fifteen, beholding the stranger's beautiful body, but he did not find her to be that good-looking. "She's more like a _____ _____," he thought. He gave her a shy wave, even as the woman was thinking that she would rather be subject to a _____ than go out with someone like him.

Returning home, Jason searched the fridge for some _____. He ate up everything he could find, and feeling bored, he started walking to a nearby _____ —a place where he would pay a little bit to be rewarded with a good night's sleep.

LEMONITIONS AND
PODGEHODGES

Lemonition

Lemonition (n)—a forewarning that a car one is about to buy is really a "lemon"

    b) for a slot player, the awful feeling of knowing that the two cherries that appear on the pay line will soon be joined by a lemon

Please Note: The term *lemonition* has now come to mean the anticipation of any negative outcome.

Sample Sentence: I had a lemonition about the new hybrid I was buying and decided to pass on it, despite the sizable rebates available.

Observation:

Why is a car that turns bad called a "lemon?" I know that lemons are sour, but the lemon is a perfectly good fruit that produces a nice little drink called lemonade.

Unlike lemons, I can't say anything remotely complimentary about prunes. In fact, why can't we use the term *prune* for a car that shrivels up and dies or for a vehicle that leaks a lot of gas? Logical?

Lesbyterian

Lesbyterian (n)—a gay female member of any organized religion

Please Note: In its original usage, the term was only used for openly gay female Presbyterians, but it is now much more ecumenical in nature.

Sample Sentence: Rhoda Robbins was delighted that her synagogue had a vibrant and welcoming Lesbyterian population.

You Know What ... ?

Usage of the term *Lesbyterian* to apply to other religions besides the Presbyterians seemed to be in common vogue starting around the 1970s. Ruth Pinkwagon, founder of the Lesybyterian Ecumenical Great Society (LEGS) related:

"It used to be that we had everyone from Latholics to Lethodists to Lews and even Lientologists all with their own groups. And then the Lesbian Lutherans did not know what to call themselves. I took the initiative to bring all of us together under a common name. This was my plan, and it's worked wonders."

Liebation

Liebation (n)—a nonalcoholic drink that is gulped from a hip flask or liquor bottle to give the appearance of being an alcoholic beverage

Sample Sentence: Not knowing that Mary was enjoying liebations from her wine bottle, Harry was constantly amazed that he was the only one of the two that was plastered.

Observation:

Liebations are often, but not exclusively, used by teenagers who want to be seen as drinking alcohol. Edward Wytelme, the longtime guidance counselor at South Pines (New Jersey) High School, provided us with the following information:

"Even before high school, we see lots of students hanging out and enjoying their liebations. Some guys, too. The problem is that they attract the attention of the local police, who are often disappointed when the would-be drunks pass the breathalyzer exam and walk straight. A secondary problem is that the power of suggestion and self-deception is strong, and many of these kids do act tipsy while liebating."

Literarity

Literarity (n)—a written work that is either unusually brilliant or, on the other hand, a piece of utter garbage

Please Note: *Literarity* can also relate to a work by a particular author that is unusually brilliant or unusually rotten—by that author's standards.

Sample Scenario: Emma reads voraciously, usually enjoying everything she picks up. For some reason, she had never found any of Stephen King's novels to be especially appealing. That all changed when she finally read *Pet Sematary*. Said Emma, "What a literarity for him; I now need to re-read all of his works to see what I've been missing." Good luck!

Observation:

Because *literarity* has two distinctly different connotations, applying it to someone's work is a little like calling a date (without the benefit of further description) "interesting." There's literarity—surprising; and literarity—disappointing.

Lollapasnoozer

Lollapasnoozer (n)—the opposite of a catnap, a lollapasnoozer is a rest on steroids. It starts out innocently enough as a twenty-minute respite but somehow morphs into an affair that may run anywhere from two hours to five days

Please Note: *Lollapasnoozer* may also refer to a person or animal renowned for taking frequent naps of various durations. A lollapasnoozer does so voluntarily; this has nothing to do with narcolepsy, or **barkolepsy** (please see entry) in the case of a dog.

Sample Scenario: I attended my very first Lollapasnoozers

International Convention and was appalled by the accommodations for the conference. For one, the agenda was so tight that they barely built in enough time for bathroom breaks, let alone nap time.

You Know What ... ?

Eighty percent of those surveyed for this edition say that they take at least one nap per day. The fifth person was still asleep when I attempted to poll her.

Macaphoney

Macaphoney (n)—a plastic representation of macaroni used to show what such a dish would look like

Secondary Meaning—a pejorative term used by pasta snobs to describe a bad plate of spaghetti

Observation:

"Yo, you want to order pasta from a diner, you get that macaphoney crap. It's like ordering shrimp from Las Vegas. Capisce?"

Ah, nothing like the wisdom set forth by my old Uncle Ned. (And, for a Jew, he really knew his macaroni—to say nothing of his shellfish.)

Just as many of my Chinese friends won't eat Chinese food from a strip mall or a food court, the same must be said about macaphoney by people who really know the good stuff. As for me, I'll tell you the truth. I love authentic Italian food, kosher food, Chinese food, etc., but I'm really not that picky, if the portions and prices are right.

Madolescent

Madolescent (n)—an irrational, crazy teenager

Sample Sentence: Needing a good, reliable babysitter for her three sons, Jessica carefully interviewed many applicants, trying to screen out all madolescents.

You Know What ... ?

Dr. Marta Hari is credited with coining this term. After counseling young teenagers privately for years, she was moved to write the following in *Young Head Cases*, her seminal scholarly work.

"I have come to the professional opinion that many adolescents, with the proper care, are completely rational, lovely young men and women. Then there is the small matter of that other 98 percent. This group is completely outside of my understanding, although they have my sympathy. I call this group *madolescents* to distinguish them from their mature, sensible peers."

Mandacious

Mandacious (adj)—dishonest—habitually lying, like a typical guy

Sample Sentence: Rachel thought she had found *the one*, but Tony proved to be just as mandacious as all the other losers she had dated recently.

Please Note: *Mandacious* is a subset of *mendacious,* the latter of which describes the untruthful actions of either a man or a woman. Yes, **womandacious** (please see entry) is the female counterpart of *mandacious.* Confused? I wouldn't lie to you.

You Know What ... ?

According to a recent poll taken by *Men Are Jerks Magazine,* mandacious behavior often concerns these five topics:

- past relationships
- current involvements
- salary/bank account
- size
- prowess

Manewer

Manewer (n)—excrement taken exclusively from male animals, which is thought to be more fertile than its female counterpart

Sample Sentence: Noticing that manewer was sold at a premium by the garden supply store, Joseph reacted as if he had just smelled a rat.

You Know What ... ?

Cletus Clever, a fourth-generation manurologist from Hurffville, New Jersey, is an expert on all kinds of natural composting material—even if he's not the most savory dinner companion. I learned that during a recent lunch interview.

Matt: Cletus, why did you decide to become a manurologist?

Cletus: I grew up on a farm, and while I didn't love manure, I respected it. My dad and his two dads—you know what I mean—were in this field before me. My mom and older sisters ran a nail salon, and I just couldn't stand the thought of being all cooped up smelling that stuff. So I wasn't what you'd call a great student, but all them facts about manure just seemed to stick.

Matt: Nicely phrased. So how do you know when to use manewer as opposed to the regular female stuff?

Cletus: From experience, I rate all types of animal feces on the bases of pungency, fertility, and productivity. Due to years of laborious studies, I only recommend manewer from the following animals—your sheep, your turkeys, and your rabbits. Stick to the female animal feces when it comes to your chicken, your cattle, your horses, and your pigs. Not only will the female stuff give you better compost, but in the right wind conditions, it will even emit a most delightful, perfume-like aroma. Say, you barely touched your chopped liver. Mind if I reach across and grab some?

Matt: Yes, I do. I mean, I'll be happy to bring some over to you. I just remembered that I'm going vegetarian this week.

Manituba

Manituba (n)—a large, loud, low-range brass instrument played in central Canada

Sample Scenario: Gordo and Whitey were getting ready to attend the championship game of their beloved Manitoba Manhunters versus the visiting Edmonton Elephants. They went over their list of things to bring to the arena. Whitey brought the face paint, and Gordo had two trusty pairs of biknockerlars. They had hoagies and chips, (just in case security would let them bring in food) and, needless to say, they had their manitubas all tuned up and ready to blast away.

Observation:

Most commonly, college football stadiums and basketball arenas are the only sports venues where brass instruments and the like are played. The manituba is an exception, as the locals—of various levels of proficiency—love to sound their instruments during hockey fights and after goals, often unnerving the visiting players in the process.

Mascary

Mascary (adj)—possessing a frightful appearance brought on by the overuse of eye shadow

Sample Sentence: After spending an hour or so in the powder room, Gena returned to her table looking positively mascary.

You Know What ... ?

Andrew Weebler is the editor of *Tasteful Eyeliners Illustrated*. He is a fount of information about proper mascara and the mascary mistakes that women (and some men) make—perhaps too much information. I decided to educate myself during a brief phone interview.

Matt: Andrew, you have a reputation within the makeup universe of telling it like it is and pulling no punches. What is some of the general advice that you give your clients?

Andrew: I always advise my clientele to avoid that mascary appearance by paying special attention to what they're putting around their eyes and lashes. They should use the proper concealer and foundations to avoid that tired, heroin-chic, goth look under the lids. That was so, like, yesterday, and—

Matt: I didn't know that the heroin-chic, goth look was *so yesterday*. Thank you—

Andrew: You interrupted me very rudely, Matthew. May I please continue? And girls, don't keep using that black eyeliner, and try to find a lighter color. Oh, avoid liquid eyeliners and stop plucking your eyebrows like a redneck playing a banjo, and ...

(*Unfortunately,* my phone got disconnected here.)

Mashticate

Mashticate (v)—crush or flatten with one's teeth

Sample Sentence: I was astonished to see Donna's little Yorkie completely mashticate her large bone.

You Know What ... ?

Denny Pendragon has an unusual hobby. He likes to analyze all types of creatures—mostly dogs—and calculate their ability to crush objects with their teeth. The ten biggest mashticaters in proportion to their weight, according to Pendragon are:

- Bichon Frise
- Wirehaired Pointed Griffon
- Finnish Spitz
- Flemish Giant Rabbit
- Peruvian Guinea Pig
- Sussex Spaniel
- Short-Tailed Opossum
- Spanish Ferret
- Miniature Pinscher
- Chinese Crested Chow Chow

Masturprobation

Masturprobation (n)—an indefinite, usually self-imposed, period of time wherein no sexual self-gratification is permitted

Sample Sentence: When Ricky flew into his bedroom with a magazine, without even stopping to smooch her or their adorable dog Smootsie, Zelda knew that he was about to end his masturprobation.

Observation:

Nah, never mind …

Mastering (*or is it, Masturing*) the Word

Masturprobation is a combination of which of the following two words:

- a. Disturb + Liebation
- b. Mastiff + Proboscus
- c. Masturbate + Rotation
- d. Masturbate + Probation
- e. Masterful + Privation

Mattresside

Mattresside (n)—the act of destroying one's sleeping cushion to the point of death

Sample Scenario:

Ricky Rotundo was well known for his inordinately long naps. He also observed long **masturprobationary** (please see entry) periods, followed by impulsive moments of self-indulgence. After concluding one of his masturprobations, Ricky went into a two-day **lollapasnoozer** (please see entry). At the conclusion of all this activity, he quite disgustingly engaged in some mattresside before calling his boss to see if his job (as a furniture salesman) was still his.

You Know What ... ?

Nita Napowski, one of the world's pre-eminent mattressologists and director of the Pillowdelphia (sorry) Mattress Society, notes, "Cases of mattresside are on the rise nationally, yet there has been a slight downturn in the number of waterbed killings. Of course, we can attribute that to the very rational fear of flooding one's home as a result."

Thanks, Rita; that's why I consult the experts.

Menerosity

Menerosity (adj)—pertaining to the readiness of freely giving—anything—to men

Please Note: Menerosity is usually, but not always, displayed by women.

Sample Sentence: Rosie was known far and wide for her menerosity—to salespeople, to charities, and to whatever lucky guys she was dating.

Observation:

Menerosity may carry a quite negative connotation, but it all depends on one's perspective. If you are a male solicitor for a charitable organization, a salesman, or just a guy out to have a good time, menerosity is a quite noble attribute.

It would appear that, given this tough economy, menerosity has been on the wane the last couple years. Of course, that is only my perspective as a salesman; I haven't dated in years (I'm married), and haven't solicited for any charitable organizations lately.

Menorahty

Menorahty (n)—the smaller part of the larger group, as describes Jews during the Christmas season

Sample Sentence: As I spun my little dreidel and lit my miniature Hannukiah, I looked over at the immense Christmas tree and felt every bit like a small menorahty.

You Know What ... ?

Per www.jewishvirtuallibrary.org (2006 data), American Jews are a distinct menorahty—and not only around the December holidays. Jews comprise only 2.2 percent of the U.S. population, ranging from 0.1 percent in several states (including West Virginia, South Dakota, and Idaho) to 5.5 percent in New York State.

While this Web site doesn't say so, it is believed that even in Idaho, 83 percent of all stand-up comedians, doctors, and lawyers are Jewish. Not sure exactly how that works, though.

Meticklish

Meticklish (adj)—thorough and attentive to great detail when it comes to tickling

Sample Sentence: While Herbie is not a great fan of being tickled, his masseuse, Sasha, is so meticklish that he finds himself visiting her on a weekly basis.

Observation:

At the risk of offering you more info than you need, I will freely admit to not being a fan of the tickle, unless I'm tickling my baby's feet or belly. But I may be out of touch with the latest trends here.

The prestigious Topeka Tickle Institute reports that tickling is now in their top ten of the most common therapeutic massage services requested by clientele. The full list is below—from most to least popular:

1. Swedish massage
2. Aromatherapy
3. Hot-stone massage
4. Shiatsu
5. Sports massage
6. Accupressure
7. **Tickling**
8. Sandpaper sampling
9. Cold-stone massage
10. Foot bashing by premenstrual therapists wielding farm implements

Midget Tsunami

Midget Tsunami (n)—a small ocean wave causing very minimal, if any, damage that has been downgraded from tsunami status

Please Note: This term has been favored by both meteorologists and surfers, albeit with different connotations. A midget tsunami is hardly an urgent meteorological event, yet those same waves are very large by surfers' standards.

Sample Sentence: "You gotta attack the midget tsunamis before they attack you, dude," was Lenny's sage advice to Ramona, the novice surfer.

You Know What ... ?

It is estimated that tsunamis date back to over three billion years ago, or approximately to around the time that Robert De Niro last made a good movie. There have also been countless midget tsunamis over the years but no terminology to qualify them as such.

(And in all fairness, De Niro still did some good work in the early '90s.)

Midwife Crisis

Midwife Crisis (n)—great psychological and emotional distress affecting women who can't find their assistant just prior to childbirth

Sample Scenario: Although Pam had her husband, George, and her doctor by her side, her midwife and confidante, Rosalita, was nowhere to be found as she was about to go into labor. She started to freak out, until George came over to reassure her. "Don't worry, dear; you're just having a little midwife crisis."

You Know What ... ?

For some, midwife crisis also has a completely different meaning. In societies that legalize polygamy, some men have three wives—known as an upper wife, a lower wife, and a midwife. The wives may be grouped that way due to chronology, geography, or where they are positioned on their bunk bed. In this scenario, and depending upon the strength of the relationship(s), a midwife crisis could have a whole host of meanings.

Misconstrudel

Misconstrudel (v)—to mistakenly eat a food thinking that it is something else—often leaving the eater disappointed or embarrassed

Please Note: Misconstrudel (n) is something eaten by mistake, because one thinks it is something else.

Sample Scenario: I misconstrudeled the oatmeal cookie for a chocolate-chip cookie and had to discreetly spit the dreaded raisins out into my napkin. Hate when that happens, especially if I compound the misconstrudel by mistaking a decoration for a napkin.

Observation:

To me, almost nothing is worse than crunching into what you *know* is a chocolate-chip cookie only to find that it was a misconstrudel and those luscious chips were really gooey raisins. The same goes for mistaking the toxic tofu for any other food that would be infinitely preferable to it.

One more thing: why aren't there more oatmeal chocolate-chip cookies on the market?

Mopedophile

Mopedophile (n)—an adult with an unhealthy attraction to children who tries to lure them onto his slow-moving vehicle

Please Note: There may be sick individuals of this type who also use cars and motorcycles, but no terminology has stuck to them.

Sample Scenario: The police department had issued an all-points bulletin for the man who was a prime suspect in the abduction of a young girl on his vehicle. Because they identified the suspect as a mopedophile, they assigned their special low-speed crisis unit to the case.

You Know What ... ?

In the 1950s, there was an infamous moped gang in Sanibel Island, Florida, that called itself Heck's Angels. Its members rode in packs, wore sensible clothing, and went on low-speed rides on the beaches, attempting to terrorize the tourists into giving them their seashells. As if that wasn't bad enough, some of the gang members even committed the unconscionable act of taking live shells home from the beach.

The town was in an uproar for a few years, and tourism fell off dramatically. Enter bicycle cop Garth Rothstein. On a cool, summer day in 1954, Rothstein caught up with Heck's Angels captain Lance Jones when he attempted to sell some of his hot shells to a few of the neighborhood kids. Jones was arrested and served two months in the town's detention center.

With the rogue leader behind bars, the Angels eventually disbanded. Upon his release, Jones repented and became a high school phys ed teacher and driving instructor. The town has been awash in serenity ever since.

Mosque-ito

Mosque-ito (n)—a pesky insect that attacks Muslims outside their place of worship

Please Note: Only the female of this species sucks the blood of their victims, who are 99.7 percent male.

Sample Sentence: Mohammed told his fellow congregants to hurry inside and pray, as the mosque-itoes were on the warpath outside the building.

You Know What ... ?

Pratekt Yussef, spiritual leader of the Eighth Avenue Mosque of Worcester, Massachusetts, relayed this lament to us:

"Our congregation is dedicated to nonviolence, and we are virulently patriotic U.S. citizens. We face some skepticism and mistrust in the greater community, but that problem has diminished recently. What hasn't diminished is our problem with all the mosque-itoes. Those little bastards (evidently, Yussef didn't realize that they're female) continually attack us—especially during Ramadan."

Mulligatiny

Mulligatiny (n)—a very small sample of spicy soup

You Know What ... ?

There is considerable debate among semanticians over the *precise* meaning of "mulligatiny." The main questions are:

- How big can a sample be, and still qualify as very small?
- How spicy does the soup need to be?

Here is the general consensus and wisdom for the above:

- The sample can only be a tablespoon or less. Yes, but rounded or heaping? Since it's hard for soup to heap on a spoon, the usual definition is *rounded*, and a heaping tablespoon of peppery soup would not qualify as mulligatiny. Now, if you are able to heap a qualified soup on a teaspoon, it's okay.

- How peppery is the soup? Does it have to be mulligatawny? No, it need not be mulligatawny, but a little curry won't hurt you. Pepper or curry does not have to dominate the palate, but your average chicken, lentil, or tomato soup does not qualify.

Nearvana

Nearvana (n)—in New Age Buddhism, the feeling of being very close to the perfect place, expressed more as a state of being than as a physical place

Sample Sentence: Xiao Lu meditated every day for fifteen years but was frustrated that he could not even attain Nearvana.

Please Note: Some of my esteemed colleagues believe that this word came into being when its inventor was so smitten with a girl named Vana that he thought it to be heaven just to be next to her. I have no reason to dispute this, as most Vanas and Vannas in my experience would seem to inspire such a yearning. Now, if the word were *Nearsadie,* I'd be much more skeptical.

Observation:

I have always felt Nearvana to be preferable to Nirvana (with apologies to Kurt Cobain, just in case) as Nirvana connotes a total peace of mind with no cravings, anger, resentments, or obsessions. I simply would not want to picture my life without these four emotional staples but would be willing to get close to that state for a little while.

Necktureen

Necktureen (n)—the fancy covered dish cannibals use to eat human parts

You Know What ... ?

Those who have already read about "cannibal lecterns" may come to the unfortunate conclusion that this author somehow advocates, tolerates, or propagates cannibalism. Nothing could be further from the truth, yet I do endeavor to present a balanced perspective on the issue. To that end, I interviewed anthropologist, Klaus Schulman.

Matt: Klaus, my researchers tell me that you have been studying cannibals for over twenty years. Sounds unsafe to me.

Klaus: Thanks for your concern, Matt, but I do keep a safe enough distance. My mentor, Georgina Rogers, taught me that just before she was tragically swall—er, I don't wish to go into that now, but let's just say I learned a lot from both her life and her tragic demise.

Matt: You have written extensively about some of the activities that cannibals enjoy. Please enlighten us.

Klaus: Most cannibals enjoy high-culture things like an art film or a good lecture. Kinky desserts sometimes follow, but at the same time, they also exhibit excellent etiquette at the dinner table.

Matt: So cannibals are usually well-mannered?

Klaus: Essentially, yes. If you look past what they eat, in my experience, cannibals are very sociable, convivial, and quite well-mannered. And they don't simply eat human body parts; they also enjoy genteel things like the occasional ice cream cone after a grueling round of miniature golf.

Matt: But what *of* the human flesh they consume?

Klaus: When they do eat human flesh, most prefer to do so more discreetly. Cannibals are known for their pot-luck dinners, where necktureens are often used to "class it up" a bit. And I've been told by many cannibals that their "mystery meat" is often very tasty.

Matt: You have written about their gala banquets. What is generally served at, say, their awards dinners?

Klaus: The works. Everything from soup to nuts.

Nightstick Figure

Nightstick figure (n)—a primitive, amateurish, black-and-white drawing, usually perpetrated by cops

You Know What ... ?

Nightstick figures have probably existed ever since the creation of municipal police departments. The most famous early practitioner of such art was Detective Randy McMillan of the New York Police Department. McMillan was confined to ten months of desk duty while he was being investigated by the Internal Affairs Department. Bored with his new mundane tasks, he began to doodle and continued the hobby until he developed a distinctive style that became quite popular with his fellow officers.

McMillan's works depicting cops apprehending criminals, shooting in self-defense, and eating donuts during stakeouts were soon hung all over the precinct. The detective even had his works featured in local art galleries, and he earned lavish praise from critics. Edna Gallows, venerable art critic for the *Old Yorker,* once said of McMillan, "Though they looked simplistic on the surface, McMillan's etchings were courageous, vivid, resonant, and stark in their imagery. His *Sugar High Stakeout* was a masterstroke of genius that had me wanting to lick the canvas and taste one of those black-and-white donuts."

Nomenculture

Nomenculture (n)—a society that doesn't recognize any achievements or contributions made by its male members

Observation:

I know that some of you are thinking, "So what?" But in all defense of my gender, you must recognize that we have had a few good representatives over the years: men like Albert Einstein, Ben Franklin, Paul Newman, Leonardo da Vinci, George Washington Carver, Babe Ruth, Dr. J, and Hugh Hefner. To whatever degree men have screwed up this planet, there have been some notable exceptions.

Truth be told, a nomenculture is more of a fictionalized society, or perhaps an ideal state to some. Anthropologists surveyed for this edition were not able to find any true examples of a thriving nomenculture—the occasional Amazonian village notwithstanding.

Sample Sentence: Ned was so chauvinistic that he feared a woman president would turn our country into a virtual nomenculture.

Obloxious

Obloxious (adj)—pertaining to a very offensive, ostentatious spread of smoked salmon

Sample Sentence: Much as I used to love Aunt Sadie's Sunday brunches, I came to feel guilty eating such obloxious amounts when I knew that people were starving just a few miles away.

You Know What ... ?

Judith Tasselberg, author of *Obloxious Brunches and Other Family Lore* (Schmaltz Press, 2008), had this to say on the subject:

"I recall every other Sunday in Yonkers at Aunt Gertie's with my parents, two older brothers, and all of my cousins. There would usually be nineteen of us at Gertie and Sol's immense mahogany table, twenty if you counted Sniffles, the Maltese. We looked forward to playing all kinds of kiddy games and embarrassing each other in our own dastardly little ways.

"So what about the food, you ask? There were enough bagels and enough mountains of lox and hills of cream cheese to feed two hundred lumberjacks. Obloxious indeed!"

Oreganovice

Oreganovice (n)—a person who sprinkles oregano on pizza for the first time

Observation:

Oregano is used to add flavor to dishes from many cultures, including Turkish, Greek, and of course, Italian. It is also an anti-oxidant (in case you thought it was a pro-oxidant) as well as an herb used for medicinal purposes.

Having said this, I mostly associate oregano with pizza, and it's hard to imagine a slice of pizza without my favorite herb sprinkled on top. When I first encountered oregano, I was at the home of my friend, Sal Palombo, and he handed me some fresh oregano leaves. Not knowing what to do with them, I immediately started folding them into patterns. I called it *oregagami*, but the Palombos were not very impressed. Since then, I try to avoid the leaves and just stick to the stuff that is ready to pour.

Call me finicky, but if I'm having pizza, I prefer it plain, well-baked (thin or thick crust), with oregano and garlic the only additions. No white pizza, no tomato pies, no toppings! Thanks for indulging me.

Ovalteen

Ovalteen (n)—an egg-shaped adolescent

Sample Scenario: Rex did not know what to expect from his first day as an eight-grader. His family had just moved into a new school district, the fourth such change he had to navigate in his young life. Would he fit in socially? Rex was an ovalteen, and within a few days, he knew that he desperately wanted to fit in with the popular, round-faced boys like Buddy Smithson.

You Know What ... ?

Our friend, Dr. Marta Hari, weighed in with this nugget:

"The external form of adolescents has a lot to do with shaping their future. Fittingly enough, the rounder the kid—to a point—the more well-rounded they will become. In other words, informal studies have shown that the shape of these kids shapes their future as well. Here is how I would rank—in descending order—how different teen shapes rank as far as well-roundedness. (Don't feel bad if you're confused here.):

1. Round teens
2. Pear-shaped teens
3. **Ovalteens**
4. Rectangulars
5. Triangular teens
6. Squares

Pachydermatologist

Pachydermatologist (n)—a doctor specializing in the skin care of elephants, rhinos, and hippos

Please Note: Although pachydermatologists are rare in the United States, pachydermatology is a thriving profession in India and parts of Africa.

Sample Sentence: When my pet rhino, Seymour, showed me a skin lesion that was making his toes itch, I immediately hitched up the trailer and took him to his pachydermatologist.

You Know What ... ?

The seven most common skin complaints handled by New Delhi pachydermatologists in 2009 were:

- Lesions of the foot
- Herpes
- Psoriasis of the trunk
- Rhinoseborreah
- Acne
- Elephant eczema
- Hippo hives

Palisthenics

Palisthenics (n)—light exercises done with a partner that are more conversational than exhaustive in nature

Sample Sentence: After a month of supposedly rigorous palisthenics with my friend, Dave, I was blubbergasted to see that I had actually gained twelve pounds.

You Know What ... ?

Heidi Littlepage, a personal trainer in Warsaw, Indiana, has devised a survey to detect if one is serious about exercise or is just in it for the palisthenics. She said that you are in the latter camp if you answer "yes" to four or more of these seven questions:

1. Are more than 80 percent of your workouts with someone else?
2. Do you frequently go out to eat immediately after exercising?
3. Do you talk more than you run or lift?
4. Do you wear clothes more for style than practicality?
5. Do you love to ride in elevators?
6. Do you consider yourself to be a Republican?
7. Are you more than twenty pounds overweight?

Pandamoanium

Pandamoanium (n)—a special place where pandas can complain and vent—away from all of the zoo visitors

Sample Scenario: Animal lovers Sven and Inga Jarlsson had traveled to China from their home in Stockholm just to visit the Beijing Zoo. Like most zoo visitors, they loved the giant pandas, but they were highly disappointed that the black-and-white cuties weren't much more active. After seeing very little in the first three hours of their visit, Inga impulsively tried to sneak into the pandamoanium, only to be stopped by a phalanx of yellow-shirted security guards.

You Know What ... ?

Li Taoxi, pandamoanium guard of the Beijing Zoo, relates the seven biggest complaints of his pandas:

- Tourists who don't speak Mandarin
- Flashbulbs
- Soggy bamboo
- Annoying cell phone ringtones
- The growing Chinese Tea Party Movement
- High unemployment rates
- Hard to find a competitive ping-pong game.

Papier-Machete

Papier-machete (n)—a weapon, made of paper fragments, wielded against very weak enemies

Sample Sentence: Roger was such a wuss that he routinely cried like a baby whenever I attacked him with my papier-machete knife.

You Know What ... ?

With apologies to Napoleon, one doesn't usually think of France as the victor in many military battles, but the most famous use of papier-machetes to secure a military victory happened in the Bordeaux region of France. Okay, it was a civil war in 1887, known as the Battle of Bourg and Blaye, two sub-regions found in Bordeaux.

Essentially, a dispute arose over whether Bourg or Blaye produced the best Merlot, and General Pierre Poisson of Blaye had absorbed a few too many insults from the imperious General LeConte Henri of Bourg. The two men engaged in some vicious glove-slapping and wine-spitting, but neither would concede the battle or the unofficial title of "Sub-Region with the Most Pleasing Merlot."

Two days later, Poisson led a group of one hundred papier-machete-wielding brutes into Henri's favorite restaurant, Le Chien Jaune Tavern. Henri's men, who numbered twenty or so, were startled to see this huge army of uninvited dinner guests, and some of them allegedly started to choke on their *fromage* (cheese) course.

Showing no mercy, Poisson yelled, "Mars en Avant!" (Onward march!), and eighty or so men advanced with their flimsy weaponry until the ambushed men of Bourg were forced to cry out, "Nous nous rendons;

votre vin ne goûte pas comme le traitement des eaux d'égout." ("We surrender; your wine does not taste like sewage treatment.")

Pleased with his triumph, Poisson shook Henri's gloved hand and offered him one of his papier-machete spears as a sign of reconciliation. The hundred or so men then sat together, enjoyed a baguette or two, and drank to their heart's content.

Parabull

Parabull (n)—an allegory so contrived that it loses all its meaning and resonance

Please Note: *Parabulls* often, but don't always, deal with religious scripture or doctrine.

Sample Scenario:

Jon was complaining to Carole about his preacher's constant use of parabulls. "First, Reverend Filcher talks about Daniel, and then he mixes him up with Samson and Jonah and whomever else he has on his mind, and it's impossible to relate to.

"The other Sunday, Filcher introduces us to a supposedly little-known biblical character named Shpilka, who was a faithful servant of God, but he was exiled to Babylonia because of his long, unkempt hair and great physical feats. While exiled in Babylonia, he was attacked by one thousand Hittites who cut his hair and threw him into a lion's den. Shpilka defeated the lions, whereupon two thousand Luddites threw him into the mouth of a whale. Despite this horrible new predicament, Shpilka never lost his faith, and the next morning, there was a dead whale ashore, killed by a miraculous slingshot."

When Carole asked him the point of the parabull, Jon said, 'I don't know; I think it was something about being faithful and keeping your hair short."

Warning:

It should be noted that frequent exposure to parabulls may lead to physical distress, including constipation, diarrhea, nausea, and vomiting. This condition is known as *parabullimia*, which ironically affects more men than women. In fact, many men who wish to gain weight steadfastly avoid going to church or synagogue.

Parabulldozer (n)—someone who falls asleep during sermons or lectures that involve weird allegories

Sample Sentence: Tom enjoyed going to church with his parabulldozer friend, Jerry, whose snores would take his mind away from the rambling sermons of his preacher.

Parking Lotke

Parking lotke (n)—a potato pancake, often eaten during Chanukah, that is consumed at an outdoor location

You Know What ... ?

The parking lotke, like a lot of traditional foods associated with the Jewish religion, started as a necessity but continued because of tradition and commerce. I discussed this with the eminent Russian Jewish scholar Boris-Yuri Fedorov.

Matt: Mr. Fedorov? Or should I call you—

Boris-Yuri: If you please, my friends call me Basha.

Matt: Basha, the former Soviet Union was quite repressive to Soviet Jews. How were you able to keep your traditions alive?

Boris-Yuri: In former Soviet Union, Jews not allowed to pray freely. We convene together in parking lots outside synagogue to partake in some parking lotkes and borscht.

Matt: For the benefit of some of my readers, what is borscht?

Boris-Yuri: Borscht is Eastern European soup taste like paint thinner. But add some sour cream, and you've got something.

Matt: So where did you used to convene?

Boris-Yuri: Was hard to celebrate with my people in those times in Moscow. We meet discreetly behind abandoned Politburo building. Natasha and Anatoly light menorah, the men spin our frozen dreidels, and Olga Greenberg bring her beautiful golden brown parking lotkes. Was tasting great, and we never got caught.

Matt: What was the toughest part of celebrating in this way?

Boris-Yuri: I think my friend, Viktor, is KGB agent.

Matt: Why do you say that?

Boris-Yuri: That schlemiel never bring applesauce.

Thanks to the bravery of Basha and his friends, parking lotkes are now enjoyed throughout the world in all kinds of weather, in total freedom—and with applesauce.

Pastafari

Pastafari (n)—a new spiritual movement whose followers adhere to the belief that pasta should be eaten for symbolic, religious, cultural, and recreational reasons

You Know What ... ?

Before putting this book together, I had only heard a little bit about the Pastafari movement and their followers—who prefer being called Pastas, as opposed to Pastafarians. I had the opportunity to sit down briefly with Pastafari scholar Tosh Kingsmon to clarify some aspects of their beliefs and culture.

Matt: Tosh, how are you today, sir?

Tosh: I prefer "Dr. Kingsmon," or simply, the more respectful "Mon." And yes, I am having a highly spiritual day.

Matt: My mistake. I was only "Toshing" with you, Mon. I am confused about the difference between the Pastas and the Rastas. Do the Pastas also believe that Haile Selassie, the last Ethiopian Emperor, was the incarnation of God?

Tosh: We are more concerned about the end of repression and the joyful expression of life on earth, outside of the wicked influences of Babylon. Our spiritual founder was a man known to his followers simply as Haile Selective.

Matt: C'mon, Mon, was that his real name? I *haile* doubt it.

Tosh: Only corrupt, evil westerners make silly plays upon words. I told you that he became known simply as Haile Selective; his real name was Buster Spillwood—not a name that screams *leadership*.

Matt: My bad, Mon. So how does the eating of pasta tie in with your spiritual beliefs, and do you only eat a certain type of pasta?

Tosh: We believe that the body—and not some brick-and-mortar Babylonian structure—is our temple. We do not corrupt our personal temples with alcohol nor corrupt our minds with capitalism, racism, and animosity. The eating of our post-ganja pasta is symbolic, religious, and cultural. After partaking in the aroma and flavor of the cannabis, we are ready to eat lots of pasta to symbolize the togetherness of our people and our love for carbohydrates.

Matt: So what type of pasta do you consume at these ceremonies, and do you only eat it when high?

Tosh: A Rasta does not use a razor or comb on his head, and we wear our hair, as you know, in dreadlocks. What did you ask me again, Mon?

Matt: What type of pasta do you eat, and do you only eat it when high on life?

Tosh: Our pasta mostly resembles our hair, and it is a spiritual combination of capellini, linguine, and pizzoccheri. I am always high on life, Mon, and that only increases my appetite.

Matt: Of course, Mon. I notice the very catchy music in the background. Is that Peter Tosh? Bob Marley? Someone else?

Tosh: No, that's Louis Prima. I thought you would recognize him.

Matt: So you guys listen to Italian music when eating pasta?

Tosh: I did it as a peaceful gesture to you because you're Italian. Me? I listen to the classics like Tosh and Marley, and my friends and I also love this new rapper named Haile High.

Matt: Do you recommend him—even for me?

Tosh: Haile, Mon.

Pastriotic

Pastriotic (adj)—motivated to eat dessert (supposedly) out of a sense of civic duty

Please Note: Simply eating a cherry pie on George Washington's birthday is not proof positive of pastriotism.

You Know What ... ?

One of the most civic-minded trenchermen I know is Gorging George Jefferson, who once told me, "Many Americans miss the eating opportunities afforded by some of the minor holidays. In the true spirit of the red, white, and blue, my typical dessert plan for various holidays is below." For those with a great love of country, and a sweet tooth to match, check out Gorging George's suggestions.

- **New Year's Day**—"Liven it up with some ice cream, cookies, and cake drowned in champagne."
- **Martin Luther King Jr. Day**—"Some fine chocolates, or a chocolate éclair. I sometimes have a dream about this day."
- **Washington's Birthday**—"I won't tell a lie; lots and lots of cherry pie."
- **Groundhog Day**—"Not sure, but whatever it is, do it over and over and over ... "
- **Valentine's Day**—"Warm your heart, your sweetie's, and your country's by eating heart-shaped chocolates."
- **Memorial Day**—"Whatever it is, make it memorable."
- **July Fourth**—"Something red like cherry pie, something white like chocolate pretzels, and add some blueberry muffins and pie as well."
- **Labor Day**—"A hard-working treat like a box of chocolate-chip cookies."
- **Columbus Day**—"Celebrate with something round, such as a pound cake, or something Spanish for that matter."

- **Halloween**—"One is never too old to trick-or-treat or to help your kids eat their candy."
- **Veterans Day**—"Many military bases sell great pastries on this day."
- **Thanksgiving Day**—"Pumpkin pie a la mode."
- **Christmas**—"Whatever your religion, pig out on some red and green cookies. What else?"
- **Weekends**—"A time for family and for thinking about our great nation. I believe the best way to honor our freedom is to celebrate each weekend day as if it's New Year's Day!"

Pastronomy

Pastronomy (n)—the study of cold cuts consumed on other planets

Sample Sentence: My pastronomy major roommate's thesis was titled "Is There Intelligent Life in Uranus, and if so, do Uranians Prefer Pastrami or Corned Beef?"

Observation:

Many American colleges are offering new fields of study in order to lower their dropout rates. One such progressive thinking institution is Slippery Slope (PA) College, where Phyllis Inonit is the admissions director. Ms. Inonit observes: "In just the last five years, we have added some innovative courses to our already world-class array of disciplines. While our department heads don't approve every single suggestion, we are proud to have licensed professors in exciting new fields such as plastic cutting, skateboard juggling, and barnyard vivisection. While pastronomy is a terrific new field, brisketology didn't make the cut."

Ouch!

Pendulummox

Pendulummox (n)—a rather stupid person who swings back and forth for no apparent reason

Please Note: A pendulummox could also be one whose opinions on various topics swings back and forth for no apparent reason.

You Know What … ?

Once again, we turn to Dr. Marta Hari for her clinical expertise.

"Most people only think of the pendulummoxes who swing back and forth in a physical manner, and some only picture the verbal type, but there are some hybrids. In fact, I had a fascinating hybrid couple named Garry and Mildred Dimwittie who visited me every Tuesday for twenty-three years. Millie was fond of shouting, 'No more abortions,' and then after twenty seconds of silence would shout, 'Abort all unwanted children.' All the while, Garry would be climbing the walls like a giant spider and swinging his legs like a lever."

When I asked Dr. Hari if she was able to cure them, she replied, "No. I came to depend upon the Dimwitties for my Tuesday entertainment. Charming people really, and they never missed a co-pay in twenty-three years."

Penetrite

Penetrite (v)—to pierce very slightly, as to be almost unnoticeable to the other party

Sample Sentence: Sammy thought he was pleasing Lucinda, only to learn years later that he had been barely penetriting her.

Observation:

Penetrite has a sexual connotation, but it also denotes anything that is pierced only slightly—everything from body parts to football defenses. When getting pierced, many teens ask that their ears (or belly buttons or eyebrows, etc.) be only penetrited enough for a small ring or pin. In football, an ineffective offense can be said to have only slightly penetrited the opposing team's stalwart defense.

Now, when it comes to sexual, um, penetrition, I will only scratch the surface of this topic. Space limitations (and space limitations alone) restrict me from exploring further.

Pennylodeon

Pennylodeon (n)—a very cheap movie or inexpensive movie theatre

You Know What ... ?

Nationwide, the average price of a single movie ticket—for a first-run film—is about $10. Typically, a pennylodeon will charge about $1.75, and sometimes the films are even worth it. Many grateful pennylodeon patrons customarily tip their ushers or feel obliged to buy an additional vat of overpriced popcorn or soda. My own local pennylodeon advertised the following films for the coming month:

- Attack of the Nymphoid Hedgehogs 3
- Santa and the Flatulent Chimney
- Mutant Cheerleaders Return to Prison
- Million Dollar Baby
- Night Zombie Versus the Catnapper
- The Wit and Wisdom of Sarah Palin and 50 Other Short Documentaries
- How to Make Your Neighbor Jealous of Your Neighbor's Neighbor

Pestuary

Pestuary (n)—a piece of land set aside for the safety and refuge of annoying insects

Sample Sentence: Not noticing the sign, John could not believe that he had to pay a fine for killing a mosquito in an official pestuary.

You Know What ... ?

For a variety of reasons, pestuaries have become very controversial, as they don't seem to work well for humans or for the pests they are designed to protect. More than 93 percent of all pests surveyed still live outside of the pestuaries, and the statistics below attest to their declining popularity:

- Biblical Locust Park of Carbon Hill, Illinois, has reported fewer visitors each year since 1986. Ironically, T-shirt sales have improved in each of the last twelve years.
- 86 percent of all visitors have admitted to illegally squashing at least one bothersome insect per visit.
- 99 percent of all such visitors complained of bites, redness, swelling, and religious infidelity.

Philantropic

Philantropic (adj)—describing the generous wasting of one's money on travel

Sample Sentence: Comparing their meager savings to their immense stack of unpaid bills, Wilma decided that she had to do something to change Norman's philantropic ways.

Observation:

It seems to your humble author that tropical vacations have much in common with either a buffet supper or sleeping with the family dog: they sound like good ideas at the time but rarely work out as planned. I have had many painful post-buffet moments and will leave it at that. When my wife and I had a dog, I often suggested that Lucky (our late cocker, who was otherwise wonderful) sleep with us, only to remember that he somehow took up the whole bed, put his butt in my face, and silently broke some deadly wind.

So why are warm-weather vacations often so catastropic? One always ends up spending more than planned and still returns home either with no tan or burnt to a crisp. And besides, there's no family dog to sleep with.

Phone Jackulation

Phone jackulation (n)—an unusual syndrome affecting thousands of Americans who get overly excited every time the phone rings

Please Note: This syndrome has nothing to do with phone sex, or pre-arranged sex dates over the phones. Scientists believe that phone jackulation is a random physiological response that occurs mostly between the hours of 2:00 AM and 10:48 PM.

Sample Sentence: Unaware that her husband suffered from phone jackulation, Tricia was very suspicious every time Randy took calls in his private study.

You Know What ... ?

Phone jackulation, while not known to be associated with any other disorder, has been informally linked to the following:

- Incidence of chicken pox prior to age fifteen
- Too much fiber and too few free radicals in the diet
- Swelling of the dominant hand's thumb and index finger

Pinochle Sandwich

Pinochle Sandwich (n)—term given to a punch in the mouth during or after a card game

Warning:

A pinochle sandwich may not occur *before* a card game, although it may occur during or after pinochle, bridge, gin rummy, "Go, Fish," etc. I'm not much of a card player, but I have heard that pinochle sandwiches are not very tasty—unless one is masochistic.

You Know What … ?

Our consultant for this entry is Festus Rosenbleeth, author of the captivating book *They Shot Card Players, Didn't They?* Here's an excerpt:

"We learned about the outlaws who were so mean that they would shoot anyone accused of cheating them at a poker game, and it made no difference whether the cheater was a man, woman, child, or cuddly pet. Yet one of the scariest figures to ever enter a saloon in the Wild West never even carried a gun. He didn't have to.

"Lefty Crenshaw was the scourge of Silver City, a drunken regular at card tables throughout the roughneck town. The 6'8" cowboy would regularly invite people over to his card game. If winning, he was a wonderful guy and would buy rounds of drinks until closing. But problems often arose as Lefty never won, and he was notorious for his horrific sense of sportsmanship.

"When losing at pinochle, he would accost whoever had the audacity to be winning the game. 'How'd you like a pinochle sandwich?' he would roar at a fellow player, and before his overmatched buddy could even answer, Crenshaw would bash him in the mouth. It seemed to work every time. The stunned player would hit the deck, only to find two or three of his teeth rolling around the floor. Invariably, the fallen player would ride over to the town dentist, and Lefty's buddy, Rotten Red Hogan, would then summon over some poor sap to take his place.

"Pleased with his success at pinochle, Lefty would later perfect a similar move at the bridge table as well, showing off his impeccable comic's timing—and thunderous left hook."

Pirouwet

Pirouwet (n)—a whirling, balletic move employed in hopes of avoiding contact with water. *Pirouwet* can also be used as a verb.

Sample Sentence: I futilely pirouwetted around the shower stall but still ended up looking like a soaked paper bag.

You Know What ... ?

Melanie "Legs" Bodoni, owner/operator of Everyday Ballet, explains why this move is so popular. "Many of our clients ask to learn the pirouwet, as it is such a versatile maneuver. While most people aren't foolish enough to try it in the shower (Thanks, Mel), it is often used outdoors to dodge raindrops, or even large puddles, in a stylish kind of way.

"The pirouwet is surprisingly easy to learn and should be mastered before trying to learn all the 'p' moves—your plies, poses, piques, pas de poisson, and the like."

Good to know.

Pizza Pi

Pizza Pi (n)—a pizza that is cut into approximately 3.14159 pieces, or anything that is divided into unusual amounts

You Know What ... ?

The pizza pi owes its origin to a small pizzeria in Cambridge, Massachusetts, called Cheesy Creations. According to local legend, a snobbish math major from MIT named Thad Smithson asked the counter girl if she could cut a pizza into 3.14159 pieces. She shot him a look and said, "Yes, if you really enjoy the value of pi so much." She proceeded to pull out her protractor and cut the pizza (allegedly, it was topped with anchovies and mushrooms) in exactly that many slices.

Thad was impressed and returned to Cheesy Creations one week later only to find that "Cheesy Creations Special Pizza Pi" was now on the menu. He protested that he should be given credit for the invention, but the girl only gave him a free soda and told him to buzz off.

Footnote: The young girl's name was Marta, and yes, she became the eminent psychologist, Dr. Marta Hari. Thad once bragged about making love to her 3.14159 times. You do the math!

Podgehodge

Podgehodge (n)—something so sloppily thrown together that it appears to be neat. A podgehodge can describe a physical space as well as a grouping of words and ideas.

Sample Scenario: Lamont is so casually brilliant that even his podgehodges blow away my own carefully measured analyses. It pisses me off.

Observation:

I have known a few people like Lamont from the above scenario. Not only are they great extemporaneous speakers, but they also have a knack of appearing to be so nonchalant about it. I'm not really sure how to put this into words, which is, admittedly, a problem for an author—and which you are now inheriting.

If only I could call Lamont over to my keyboard. He would slap some ideas together, call it "My Observation," and we would all be left shaking our heads (and hopefully, they wouldn't rattle too loudly) at his artistry.

REVIEW OF FIRST 150

1. Phone jackulation has been informally linked to:
   a. too much fiber in the diet
   b. swelling of the dominant hand's thumb and index finger
   c. incidence of chicken pox prior to age fifteen
   d. all of the above
   e. none of the above

2. The Battle of Bourg and Blaye featured which of the following:
   a. the strategic use of papier-machetes
   b. spirited wine-spitting
   c. vicious glove-slapping
   d. all of the above hyphenated tactics

3. Which instrument is commonly played from the stands at central Canadian hockey rinks?
   a. the kazoo
   b. the mandolin
   c. the manituba
   d. the clockenspiel

4. According to a leading anthropologist, what are cannibals famous for eating at their gala affairs?
   a. strawberry bilkshakes and peanut butter
   b. a prudent sampling of Danish
   c. mulligatiny
   d. everything from soup to nuts

SNORGANIC POPSICKLES

Popsickle

Popsickle (n)—short for "Pop's sickle," an implement reserved for the family patriarch and used for cutting grain or tall grass

Please Note: This word comes to us from Russia, where people have always had a great reverence for their semi-circular bladed tools, as well as for their fathers. No, there's no *pophammer.*

You Know What ... ?

Mikhail Jordan, professor of field clearing at Odessa (Russia) A&M, is the author of a dynamic new book entitled *Watching My Father's Tools: A Memoir.* It was an honor to interview him, even if I couldn't tell whether his sense of humor was very poor or very advanced.

Matt: Professor Jordan, has Russian culture always been so reverential about farm implements and the protocol of who should use them?

Professor Johnson: Relentlessly so. For many centuries, Mother Russia has always been a very patriarchal society that also places great emphasis, and even reverence, over these implements. The father has always been accorded the honor of leading the way in the wheat fields, and he wields the most ornate and sharpest sickle, which has come to be known as the popsickle. The first son inherits his Dad's tool; if no male sons are born, the sickle is buried with the old man.

Matt: Isn't it ironic that *Mother Russia* is so patriarchal?

Professor Johnson: No, I don't see the irony.

Matt: Mother Russia. (pause) Still nothing? My mistake. But tell me, sir, where are the daughters in all this? Do they ever get to use their father's prized tools?

Professor Johnson: In very rare cases, yes. For instance, a farm girl from outside Vladivostok named Katya inherited Anatoly Pasternacky's tool in 1983.

Matt: Did this event shatter the glass ceiling for Russian farm girls?

Professor Johnson: Apparently not, but I'm sure that it helped young Katya harvest some wheat.

Porcinema

Porcinema (n)—a movie that deals mostly with swine

Please Note: A porcinema could also refer to a movie theatre that mostly shows films about pigs. Because a football is known as a pigskin, some porcinemas do show movies such as *The Longest Yard.* Your better porcinemas show the original, and not the remake.

Sample Sentence: I went to my local porcinema to see *Babe*, expecting to dread it, but I came out raving that the title character was the most entertaining pig to hit the silver screen since Porky.

Observation:

My own list of underrated porcinema classics would have to include—in no particular order:

- *Hog Rolling on the Mississippi*
- *Pig Blanket Bingo*
- *The Razorback's Edge*
- *Pig Trouble in Little China*
- *My Darling Clemenswine*
- *Days of Swine and Noses*
- *My Pig's Fat Greek Wedding*

Postentious

Postentious (adj)—the highest level of pseudo-sophisticated behavior—pretension on steroids, if you will

Please Note: As *post-modern* is to *modern*, so is the relationship of *postentious* to *pretentious*. This baffles certain semanticians, who believe *postentious* should mean the opposite of *pretentious*, something like "down-to-earth." What can I say? They are wrong.

Sample Sentence: Leo expected his blind date, Francesca, to be down-to-earth, but her constant name-dropping, label-wearing, and author-quoting indicated to him that she was a postentious bore.

Observational Musing:

Is the fact that I now find fewer things postentious a sign of: a) the world changing; b) my being more tolerant; or c) my own, um, postentiousness?

Thou shalt discuss this over the scented fruit drink of thy choice.

Postvaricate

Postvaricate (v)—to attempt to counteract a lie with a lesser lie (or sometimes even the truth) in an effort to come clean

Observation:

In many respects, a postvaricator is more ethical than a prevaricator. The latter just lies without any conscience, while the former at least makes the effort to cover his/her tracks in order to set the record straight. Another difference between the two ... varicators? The prevaricator will insist on repeating the same lie, sometimes without even realizing it. The postvaricator will start with a lie, and when his conscience kicks in, may even resort to telling the truth, often preceding it with, "I can't lie to you."

Sample Scenario: I was about to buy the used blue Honda
from Rudy's Hot Rods when I asked the proprietor how many previous owners it had. "Just one," replied Rudy. Noticing my arched eyebrows, he postvaricated, "I can't lie to you. It's had three or four, but they all spoiled it like a newborn baby, and none of them ever got a ticket or even exceeded the speed limit."

Pouch Potato

Pouch Potato (n)—slang for a certain marsupial that seems to do nothing but lie around all day in the Australian bushes. Sometimes known as **pouch tomato.**

Sample Sentence: Because Matilda was taking a short nap, Rob, the judgmental young zoologist, mistakenly took her (a normally industrious kangaroo) to be just another pouch potato.

You Know What ... ?

Enter Sheila Goolagong, Australia's most famous marsupiologist. "Why do people think that most marsupials are pouch potatoes? There are over 140 species of marsupials indigenous to Australia, and almost none of them are as lazy as human beings. We have boxing kangaroos, digging koalas, fearsome wombats, numbats and bandicoots, and acrobatic bilbies. I challenge you to find any of them just lounging around and watching the telly. Never happens on my watch. Never."

Preditation

Preditation (n)—the act of thinking deeply about attacking someone—physically, verbally, or financially

Sample Sentence: Mortgage banker Stanley Stavish engaged in deep preditation each morning before meeting with his hapless clients.

You Know What ... ?

Dirk Hargrave, author of *You Stalking to Me?* lists the ten animals that exhibit the most preditation before killing, along with his explanations.

- Meerkat—No mere cat; she's dangerous!
- Otter—Otterly scary
- Fox—Sly, intellectual and thorough
- Raccoon—Friendly by day, deadly by night
- Lynx—Don't let those tufted ears fool you
- British blue cat—Red eyes and scary accent
- Badger—Harass, burrow, and destroy
- Brown-nosed coati—Frickin' brown-noser!
- Asiatic jackal—Devious and brilliant!
- Homo Sapiens—You and me, brother

Prestifidgetation

Prestifidgetation (n)—a show of physical clumsiness that detracts from an otherwise magical performance

Sample Sentence: The Magnificent Morley wowed the crowd by pulling three doves from his chef's hat and then proceeded to spoil it with an act of prestifidgetation—tripping headfirst over the table.

You Know What ... ?

The term *prestifidgetation* is attributed to Lana Luteki, an entertainment reporter for the *Wheeling Wrapper*. Covering a magic show by the Great Screwgini in 1975, she wrote:

"The famous magician wowed those in attendance at the Wheeling Coliseum by sawing a very shapely model into three pieces. Screwgini then spun his magical case around, and the (now intact) lovely redhead took a bow to thunderous applause. He motioned for her to join him and attempted to hug her, but in an act of unprecedented prestifidgetation, he clocked her in the nose with his forearm. This elicited groans from both the redhead and the shocked crowd."

Prison Cellophane

Prison Cellophane (n)—a thin, transparent cellulose material used by certain prisoners to keep dry

Sample Sentence: Gordo, who only had five months left to serve of his twenty-year sentence, was desperate to receive enough prison cellophane to last him for the duration of his stay.

Observation:

Surveys suggest that the use of prison cellophane is a rather recent phenomenon that has not yet become too widespread. It appears that a majority of inmates still prefer the comfort of terry cloth. Bumper Morton, who served ten years in Talladega (Alabama) Federal observed:

"Man, some of these young dudes think they're cool with their prison cellophane and sh*t. Me? Just get me the luxurious comfort of ring-spun cotton. Breathable, absorbent, and pleasing to the touch. Made my stay go quick, man."

Proboscuous

Proboscuous (adj)—characterized by a lack of discrimination when it comes to noses

Sample Sentence: Marci did not consider herself to be proboscuous, yet she dated lots of men (of various nose types) and has undergone five nose jobs in the last ten years.

You Know What ... ?

Dr. Samuel Snoutenberg, chief rhinoplastic surgeon at Beautiful Beaks Boutique and Surgery Center, discusses five of the most interesting nose jobs that he advertises but rarely performs:

- **The Hockey Fighter Look**—"Daring and bold, but not for everyone."

- **The Indian Elephant Trunk**—"Once requested by a forensics expert, it helped him solve cases but was bad for his love life."

- **The Early Morning Clogger**—"Some of my patients don't like to wake up able to breathe freely, as they enjoy the whole process of clearing out the schnozz."

- **The Karl Malden**—"Great actor and owner of a distinctive honker, the late, great Malden used to inspire more imitators."

- **The Barbra Streisand**—"I used to warn them that they could look like Babs, but I could not guarantee that they would be able to sing like her. Some women, and even a couple men, signed the disclosure forms and stubbornly went through with it anyway."

I tried to set Snoutenberg up by asking him, "How do your patients pay for these procedures?" Expecting him to say "through the nose," the doctor calmly replied, "Most use credit cards, but we prefer personal checks."

Prognocrastination

Prognocrastination (n)—a prediction made *after* an event has already taken place

Please Note: *Prognocrastination* sits (and sits and sits) at the intersection of *prognostication* and *procrastination*. I'd like to be able to tell you that prognocrastinators always get their predictions right, but please see below.

You Know What ... ?

Born in 1910, Harry Honto is still a prognocrastinator of some repute. The Manchester, New Hampshire journalist has achieved notoriety for making stunningly accurate predictions after the fact. Honto, nicknamed Hindsight Harry, insists that all of his prognocrastinations have come within one week of the event, and since the paper he writes for is published bi-weekly, he has never missed a deadline in seventy-five years. Below, as a special service to this edition, Harry recounts five of his most famous predictions and even dares to look ahead.

1948—Truman Defeats Dewey: "Right up against deadline, I called this one just days after the election. The *Chicago Tribune* famously blew this one with their "Dewey Defeats Truman" headline. Well, I got it right, got it on deadline, and was within five electoral votes of a perfect prognocrastination."

1969—Miracle Mets Win the World Series: "Everyone had the Baltimore Orioles sweeping the World Series over the upstart Metropolitans, but they rushed to judgment. There was something about that Mets team that had me picking them just hours after they stunned the favored Orioles. One regret: I had them winning in six, but they did it in five."

1985—Coca-Cola Will Release "New Coke" Formula: "Some prognocrastinators *still* have not made this prediction, and it was quite shocking back in the day. Even now. I still have unopened cases of the stuff."

1990—Buster Douglas Upsets Mike Tyson: "The fight happened on February 11, in Japan, yet I got it right for our Valentine's Day edition. Not only that, but within months of this fight, I prognocrastinated that Tyson would have a lot of personal issues and would possibly serve time in jail. I also said that Buster Douglas would be an all-time great champion, so you can't win them all. Whatever happened to him, anyway?"

2001—George W. Bush Will Butcher the English Language: "I'm particularly proud of this one. Many of my colleagues claimed that "W" would go down in history as our most eloquent president. I begged to differ and predicted that he would commit many malapropisms and various misstatements. Even his *nucular* family came to agree with me."

Harry generously consented to go out on a limb (well, maybe out on a sturdy branch) and look ahead to 2010 and beyond with various predictions—in sports, politics, and world trends.

Sports: "A little-known young golfer named Eldrick (Tiger) Woods will win a lot of majors and will one day be considered one of the greatest golfers of all time, in addition to being a wonderful husband … Roger Federer will break Pete Sampras's Grand Slam career total … That Albert Pujols kid will be a good baseball player and make an all-star team or two."

Politics: "Although I may not live to see it, there will be a female president of the United States, but an African American man will get to the White House first."

World Trends: "While world population is decreasing, at least one million babies will be born worldwide next year."

Thanks, Harry. You heard it here first—sort of.

Prolechariot

Prolechariot (n)—a means of transportation often utilized by the working class

Please Note: This term is often used derisively by those who consider themselves to be superior because they drive a newer, bigger, more expensive set of wheels.

Observation:

A prolechariot is not your father's (or your favorite ancient Roman's) chariot. As such, it's a little easier to tell what it isn't than what it is.

Allow me to attempt to do so:
A prolechariot is a car that is at least one year old, though exceptions can be made if it's beat up a little or if it's one of the lowest-priced cars on the market. Most often, it's at least five years old and was never expensive to begin with. A prolechariot is not necessarily a military vehicle, and it probably was not manufactured in Russia. It's just a sensible, reliable car—most of the time.

Some (idiots) say that "you can tell a lot about a man by the car he drives." Being much more open-minded, I say that you can sometimes tell a lot about a person's car if you examine the car he drives.

Prolitteration

Prolitteration (n)—the abundance of great amounts of rubbish spread across an area

b) twelve or more kittens born in one single birth

Sample Scenario: Sally loved her tabby, Greystone, but was frightened of the cat's great prolitteration for good reason. Tabby was only ten years old and had already given birth to 150 kittens.

You Know What ... ?

Greta, an Abyssinian from Lincoln, Nebraska, is supposedly the greatest living example of prolitteration. Nicknamed "The Decapo-Mom" for her tendency to produce litters of ten or more, she has averaged three litters of ten each per year for the last twelve years. If you're scoring at home, that's 360 kittens—and she has hinted that she ain't done yet.

Proteen

Proteen (adj)—advocating the rights of your adolescent children on the assumption that it's good for your health

Sample Sentence: Dina hated the fact that her husband, Jesse, was so proteen that he allowed their girls to drink and violate curfew whenever they wanted.

You Know What ... ?

I consulted Dr. Marta Hari, author of *Young Head Cases*—a runaway bestseller in her hometown. "Too many parents give in to their obnoxious **madolescents** (please see entry), thinking that their proteen behavior will make life easier for them. It may make them feel that way in the short term, but the following common proteen stances could backfire on them big time:

- not imposing curfews
- letting them drive—at all
- cell phones before age fourteen
- credit card access
- reasoning with them—whatsoever."

Prunedoggle

Prunedoggle (n)—a wasteful government project that still exists even after the money to support it has dried out

Sample Sentence: Senator Practomyre lobbied hard against the proposed milk pipeline, arguing that it would be just another costly prunedoggle.

You Know What ... ?

Three of the biggest prunedoggles in U.S. history were:

- 1949—The state of Wisconsin allocates $25.7 million to research how to make their own Swiss cheese.
- 1973—Congress passes a bill requiring $500 million to be spent each year to study if there's a correlation between lack of television and too much sleep.
- 1962—The state of New Jersey approves $92 million to study why the state has an inferiority complex. It allocates $82 million to a PR firm in New York and the other $10 million to a Pennsylvania psychiatrist.

Psycho-Semitic

Psycho-Semitic (adj)—pertaining to an emotional disorder in which the affected person feels that he really is Jewish

Sample Sentence: Brady O'Callahan, a seventh-generation Irish American and first-generation psycho-Semite, insisted on going to synagogue every Yom Kippur.

You Know What ... ?

Gersh Lewin is known as the Renaissance Rabbi, as among other things, he's a rabbi, psychiatrist, and lawyer and competes in triathlons on alternate Sundays. He shared this tidbit about psycho-Semitism:

"There are a few—very few—people out there who suffer from psycho-Semitism. They are not Jewish, but they refuse to convert, claiming that they are already a 'member of the tribe.' It really doesn't bother me, but it's a curious thing.

"One of my patients, named Guiseppe Guido de Bolletarino (his real name is longer, but I'm respecting doctor-client privilege), used to come to my synagogue every Saturday and eat a corned beef special with cream cheese and Genoa salami while we read from the Torah. As if that weren't bad enough, after every third bite, he would exclaim, 'Oy, is that the *mechaya*!' ('So good, it's almost orgasmic'). When I asked him to stop, he accused me of being anti-Semitic. Imagine that!"

I just did.

Pumperdime **

Pumperdime (n)—a ridiculously overpriced loaf of bread

Sample Sentence: The new, fancy bakery had great products, but Mallory stopped going, as they had too many pumperdimes on display.

Observation:

A pumperdime does not have to be a loaf of pumpernickel. In fact, research has shown that pumpernickel is usually priced more reasonably than most other varieties. Informed by research, prejudice, and personal taste, I consider these to be among the common examples of pumperdimes:

- **Multigrain bread**—Do we have to pay for each and every grain?
- **White bread**—Too costly at any price.
- **Raisin bread**—Ich! See comment for white bread; I don't get why people eat this.
- **Focaccia**—A nice bread, but severely overpriced, and too hard to spell or pronounce.

** An even more expensive loaf of bread is sometimes referred to as a pumperquarter.**

Punndit

Punndit (n)—an expert practitioner of plays on words, quips, and witticisms

Punnditry (n)—expertise in the art of word play, quips, and witticisms

Punn-jab (n)—a sharp pun made by an Indian or Pakistani wordsmith

Rapunn-zel (n)—a pun—usually spoken in German—that can be either hair-raising, hair-lowering, or rather *Grimm* (Brothers!).

Pun-satawney Phil (n)—according to legend, a groundhog that sees the shadow of its own pun and decides to crawl back into its hole for six more weeks

Observation:
Okay, that's enough punn-ishment—for now.

Punnitive

Punnitive (adj)—relating to correctional discipline meted out by means of a series of terrible plays on words

Sample Sentence: While I am sure that most readers will love this book, I am aware that it may have a punnitive effect on others.

You Know What ... ?

Larry Lockwood, a Criminal Justice professor from Slippery Slope College, notes:

"Many states have outlawed punnitive measures after complaints were voiced that recipients of such treatment groaned much too loudly. It led to unrest and conflicts among the prison population.

"On the other hand, there are some advocates of punnitive measures who believe in institutions such as the punnal colony. Although I consider myself a punndit in this field, I have not yet staked out my own opinion and do not wish to punntificate further."

Pyropractor

Pyropractor (n)—a doctor who manipulates the spine of a patient, causing his/her primal urge to light the patient on fire

Please Note: A pyropractor is sometimes referred to as a chiromaniac.

Sample Scenario: Dara went into Dr. Brillo's office with her coupon for a free consultation. The doctor put her at ease about his practice and directed her to go into room three for an adjustment. Dara was feeling good about her choice of chiropractor and started to disrobe—until she noticed three fire extinguishers in the room. Fearing that the good doctor might be a pyropractor, she was about to leave as Brillo entered the room.

You Know What ... ?

The Bureau of Alcohol, Fire and Holistic Medicine reports that there have been 1,238 doctors convicted of chiromania during the last decade.

Randomonium

Randomonium (n)—a riot or disturbance that breaks out for no apparent reason

Sample Scenario: Jacob's mom warned him not to go into the city on Saturday night. "With all those people clustered around the clubs, there is likely to be a randomonium. Jacob tried to reassure her. "No, it won't be a randomonium at all; I'll be taking part in an organized riot."

You Know What ... ?

Paging Dr. Mata Hari once again: "When you have a ton of young people all bunched together, there is bound to be a number of disturbances, and even riots. In fact, it only takes one or two youths to make trouble."

Dr. Hari also quibbles when the term *randomomium* is applied to these situations. "For no apparent reason?! Ten or more teenagers?! That's reason enough for me to stay away."

It's always so reassuring to get her positive spin on things.

Rappist Monk

Rappist Monk (n)—a member of a close-knit band of hip-hop artists who live together, share musical inspiration, and make several promises, including a "vow of noisiness"

Observation:

I know that many of us confuse Rappist Monks with Trappist Monks. Here are two notable differences.

The Trappists date back to 1664, as a reform movement started in La Trappe Abbey, in Normandy, France. They are now a contemplative religious order of the Roman Catholic Church, following the Rule of St. Benedict.

The Rappists got started in 1973 in the Bronx, New York, due to the eclectic vision of Maurice "Little M" Flash. They are now a secular order of Hip-Hop Nation.

The Trappist Monks may not take a true vow of silence, but they are quiet when eating and only speak when they deem it absolutely necessary.

The Rappist Monks *only s*peak when not sleeping.

Rectanglican

Rectanglican (adj)—of, or pertaining to, the four-sided shape of certain English churches

Sample Sentence: Desmond, a bit of an architectural snob, quit his Rectanglican Church when he saw the design of a cool new place of worship a couple of blocks away.

Observation:

Not every place of worship will be as distinctive looking as Paris's Notre Dame or the Sagrada Familia in Barcelona. But Dr. Hiram Welker, who studies such things for a living, notes something very interesting:

"In a worldwide study of those who consider themselves regular churchgoers, the outward design of the place of worship was mentioned as the fourth most important factor in choosing their spiritual home."

The top three factors were:
- ease of parking
- familiarity with the service
- cost

Design finished just ahead of factors such as:
- admiration for spiritual leader
- social/educational programs
- cleanliness of bathrooms

Remorse Code

Remorse Code (n)—a system of alternating light and sound waves that is used to decipher whether someone is being truly remorseful

You Know What ... ?

The Remorse Code, developed around February 2006, is used especially in the following situations:

- domestic disputes
- political scandals
- Yom Kippur repentance

Observation:

So how *does* one tell if someone is truly being remorseful or just saying all the right things to stay in their marriage or keep political or other career viability? "We can't," says Jed Garza, inventor of the Remorse Code. "However, our lights and sound waves are triggered by certain contrivances that scream *fake remorse,* including:

- poor reading of prepared statements
- having the wife silently by the side
- the amount of sweat in the palms, forehead, and buttocks."

Remutt Control

Remutt Control (n)—a hand-held device used by owners to track and control the movement of their canine pets

Please Note: Remutt controls are still relatively new, and results of their effectiveness vary greatly.

Sample Sentence: Dylan did not realize that he had no batteries in his remutt control, so he kept clicking in vain as his golden lab, Prusha, kept running farther away.

Warning:

According to Dave Robutnik, owner of Control-Pooch, the leading maker of remutt controls, his best clickers now work with the following degrees of effectiveness:

- Calling dogs for meals—98 percent
- Muting barks—73 percent
- Getting dogs to return home—55 percent
- Stopping fights with cats—43 percent
- Eliminating hydrant peeing—25 percent
- Stopping footwear chomping—7.6 percent

Retissue

Retissue (v)—to use, or offer to someone else to use, a portable "snot rag" or piece of toilet paper for the second time

Sample Sentence: While stranded on Herman's toilet seat without any toilet paper, I could not believe that the cheap bastard retissued me only a small square.

You Know What ... ?

Mary Lou Cavette, author of *Almost Wearing Out Your Welcome*—a great guide to staying with people for free—devoted a whole chapter to putting up with subpar bathrooms. Here is a crucial excerpt from that chapter:

"Much as I love a free stay, if my hosts do not provide enough toilet paper for my potential needs, I'm out of there. It's okay to be retissued once, but if this happens more than once on the same stay, I suggest that you hightail it out of there and find another home to share your bounty with."

Share your bounty with?!

Retrosexual

Retrosexual (n) or (adj)—a person (or characteristic of such person) who is no longer sexually active

Sample Sentence: Rona was frightened of getting married because so many of her married friends had settled into a retrosexual lifestyle.

You Know What ... ?

Dr. Ivo Batowsky (partner of Dr. Marta Hari), an expert on retrosexual behavior, had this to say on the topic:

"Retrosexuality is in line with that old saying, 'The older I get, the better/smarter/stronger/faster/sexier I used to be.' Many of my patients are retrosexuals, and in most of these cases, I recommend memory-erasure therapy instead of techniques to rekindle their sex lives. That may sound mean, but a great percentage of these people and couples are beyond the reawakening phase, so my solution is to get them to stop thinking about a past that they won't be able to duplicate. It is slightly cruel but greatly effective!"

Rheummate

Rheummate (n)—an arthritic person who shares one's living space

Sample Sentence: Although Murray was ecstatic to have a new rheummate, it was admittedly a pain in the neck to help Otto tie his shoes and slurp his oatmeal.

Warning:

Rheumatoid arthritis is a very serious disorder causing pain, stiffness, and swelling in various joints. It afflicts more women than men, and for *real* information, please consult a source other than this one.

You Know What ... ?

According to a very recent survey, the most common requests made by rheummates were:

- Help with opening jars
- Tying and untying shoes
- Assistance with making paper airplanes and fortune tellers
- Origami help and critique

Robotany

Robotany (n)—the science of memorizing—in a robotic fashion—all kinds of arcane details about plants

Observation:

I can still recall my freshman year in college, when I roomed with a robotany major. My roommate, Keith, used to wake up in the middle of the night and start chanting various facts about plants. If I remember correctly, Keith's 3:00 AM incantations would go like this:

> Stems, leaves, flowers, roots, buds, fruits, and seeds
> Learning shapes of leaf blades is what I really need
> linear, elliptical, ovate
> lanceolate, cordate
> apex, acuminate
> sagittate, and truncate.

Still catchy all these years later! After spewing out more robotanical facts, Keith would invariably clear his throat five times and go back to sleep. I, on the other hand, would be up all night. We roomed for about two months, and then I petitioned for a new roommate. For the balance of the semester, I shared a dorm room with a flatulent oboe player. So be careful what you wish for.

Rodentistry

Rodentistry (n)—a highly specialized field of medicine concerning the proper dental care of nibbling mammals

You Know What ... ?

I am proud to call Dr. Woodrow Thorenson a friend. "Thorsie" has enjoyed a thriving rodental practice for over thirty years. Below is an excerpt from an interview I conducted with him.

Matt: Dr. Thorenson, who or what are your patients?

Thorsie: I am fortunate to have quite a varied, eclectic clientele: everything from beavers to muskrats to chipmunks and squirrels, and my personal favorite, the lemmings. Do you want to know why they are my favorite?

Matt: Okay, I'll bite.

Thorsie (wincing a little from the pun): You take care of one lemming, and the rest of them just seem to follow. Cuts down on marketing expenses.

Matt: Are there any types of clients you are not too fond of?

Thorsie: Of course. I'm not a great fan of the porcupine. They are very fussy, and dare I say—

Matt: Prickly?

Thorsie: Bingo. And I must put in a good word for that beautiful animal—the beaver. It's always a pleasure to see lots of beaver in my waiting room. There is one downside, though.

Matt: Really?

Thorsie: Every beaver I know is a nocturnal creature. It messes up my office hours, and I have to pay a shift differential and overtime to my rodental hygienists and office staff.

Matt: Never thought of that. Dr. Thorenson, do you have any advice for those thinking about a career in rodentistry?

Thorsie: Let me chew on that a moment. Yes, I do. Forty percent of the world's mammal population is rodents, and they really use their teeth, so it's a great field. Just study hard, get lots of cheap, easy-clean furniture, and get ready to do battle with the insurance companies.

Romadic

Romadic (adj)—describing a person who is at his/her most romantic when wandering away from home

Sample Sentence: Jealous Jimbo was wary of his wife's business trips, which he felt were just Natalie's excuses to enjoy some romadic adventures.

You Know What ... ?

Akant Kipstilla, a Bedouin psychologist, considers himself somewhat of an expert on romadic adventures. "Most of my people are constantly on the go, partly because of our economy and the condition of the dry lands in which we live, and mostly because all this movement makes the women among us more amorous." For real?

"Yes." (That explains it.) "As a fifth-generation camel breeder, my family name carries with it a certain prestige. And on top of that, being a psychologist who does tent calls, I get my choice of the ladies." So does he frequent the Bedouin and Breakfast establishments? "No, there's not enough privacy there. There are better, secretive places to go."

Hmm ... maybe, we'll get his advice for volume two?

Romanitarian

Romanitarian (adj)—showing concern for and helping to improve the welfare and happiness of others by offering free sexual favors

Observation:

Romanitarian is a highly subjective term. Many of those who believe that they are performing romanitarian acts are somewhat delusional, as they are actually the recipients of such largesse.

Sample Sentence: Brenda took such pride in being a romanitarian to men in need that she listed it on her resume as a special accomplishment.

Please Note: A majority of surveys of American religious institutions shows that most romanitarian acts are not committed by clergyman— they are engaged in by lay leaders.

Rooster-Pecked

Rooster-pecked (adj)—intimidated and abused by one's husband

Please Note: This term is usually used in societies or cultures where the woman is usually dominant or at least on equal footing with her spouse.

Sample Scenario: Amanda the Amazonian had very little sympathy for her rooster-pecked friend, Lily. "Get the hell away from him now, or let him deal with me," she would tell her.

You Know What ... ?

Below is my interview with Ron Rhombus, president of Seattle's chapter of Rooster Peckers Anonymous.

Matt: Ron, what is the mission of Rooster Peckers Anonymous?

Ron: Very simple, Matt. We dedicate ourselves to privately helping men become less domineering husbands.

Matt: How many members do you have?

Ron: We're anonymous. We help a lot of people. Okay?!

Matt: Approximately how many?

Ron: Wish I could tell you. What else you got?

Matt: Okay then, how does your program work?

Ron: We have a twelve-step program that transforms our crowing, abusive roosters into gentle doves, but we do so in a way that preserves our dignity.

Matt: Do any of the roosters become like capons in the process?

Ron: We only do twelve steps. That's the thirteenth step, you &&%^-ing nitwit!

Matt: Thank you, Ron. You sound like a changed man.

Runaway Model

Runaway Model (n)—a person employed to exhibit fashion who suddenly escapes from a catwalk or photo shoot to pursue other interests

Please Note: The term *runaway model* conjures up images of beautiful ladies literally flying off the catwalk to places unknown. In point of fact, only 13 percent of all runaway models desert the catwalk; the great majority of runaway models disappear during outdoor location shoots.

You Know What ... ?

Perhaps the most notorious runaway model of them all was the beautiful but mysterious Greta (Missing) Persson. Greta, a gorgeous, blue-eyed brunette from Stockholm, appeared on many magazine covers in Europe and was on the verge of great fame in the United States when she abruptly ran away during a swimwear shoot in the 1980s.

Photographer Antonio Farfellino still recalls the day Ms. Person left modeling so abruptly. "I was in charge of a very important shoot for *Popular Thongs* magazine, and we were delighted to have Greta pose for our double swimsuit issue. Well, one moment I'm complimenting Ms. Persson on a gorgeous turquoise number she was wearing, and the next thing I know, she's telling me, 'I don't want to wear this piece of crap. Please leave me alone.'"

"I was stunned. This issue would have catapulted her, and us, to great international fame and fortune. Anyway, she told me she wanted to think about it some more. Long story short, I told her she could take a two-hour break. Next thing I know, she leaves the area in some sort of kooky disguise, and she never did another photo shoot for us, or anyone, again.

"It's a shame, really," adds Farfellino. "She was the most breathtakingly beautiful woman I've ever photographed, and now she's simply known in the industry as "Missing Persson.""

Sargasm

Sargasm (n)—an apparent instance of powerful physical and emotional relief that is feigned in order to send a derisive message to the other party

Please Note: As a newer wordapod, semanticians are still wrestling with the exact definition of *sargasm*. As this volume went to press, my crack research team was not able to consult with experts, including staff members of the prestigious Pullman Institute of Unusual Pleasures.

However, this much seems to be known about this entry:

- Its adjectival form is either *sargasmic* or *orcastic*
- It is not to be confused with *sourgasmic*, defined here as "a powerful pleasurable relief that takes a distasteful turn."
- It is also not to be confused with an *orcasm,* defined as "one whale of a sexual climax."

Sample Sentence: Simon was devastated when he discovered that Mona's pleasurable screams were entirely sargasmic in nature.

Shaviation

Shaviation (n)—the art of shaving in the bathroom of a moving aircraft

Sample Sentence: Glenn's shaviation ability was so advanced that he entered the airplane bathroom with a full beard and returned to his seat six minutes later with nary a trace of stubble.

You Know What ... ?

Most of you have no doubt heard about the legendary Mile High Club, and some of you may even be members. The Mile High Club honors those who have engaged in sexual relations while flying, but there is no certification available—leading me to believe that many *members* have only engaged in **fictionary** (please see entry) behavior.

A somewhat different club is the Society for International Speed Shaviators (SISS), which honors those who have performed great feats in shaviation. After much controversy, SISS allowed the Women's Association of Leg and Armpit Shavers (WALAS) to be a part of their group in 1997. Indeed, the acronym *SISS* fits them well. Brynn Stubblemire is president of the SISS Hall of Fame in Pawtucket, Rhode Island. Per Stubblemire, here are three watershed moments in shaviation history.

June 10, 1905—Two years after wowing the world near Kitty Hawk, North Carolina, Wilbur Wright enjoyed a longer flight, taking off from Dayton, Ohio, and staying in the air for thirty-nine-plus minutes and close to twenty-four miles. Brother Orville teased him that he was up so long that he needed to shave, and Wilbur blamed himself for not bringing a razor with him.

November 3, 1952—Passenger Gareth Murray brought a safety razor aboard one of the first ever BOAC flights from London to Johannesburg. He was said to have done a respectable job of shaving off his handlebar mustache before the plane (a DC-3) crashed and burned. His famous last words were, "Well, there's twenty minutes I'll never get back."

August 28, 1959—Richie Greenstein was the first to use an adjustable razor successfully on an international flight. Flying on Pan Am from London to New York, Greenstein asked his wife, Nora, to stand outside the bathroom door and time him. Exactly eight minutes and five seconds later, Greenstein came out looking like a mensch, to which Nora commented, "You gonna wear those trousers to your own father's funeral?!"

Shingull

Shingull (n)—a coastal bird distinguished by both its majestic flight and its propensity to attack signs outside doctor's and lawyer's offices

Sample Sentence: Brandon Jones, Esq., had a dilemma: he was proud of the sign announcing his practice but dismayed by all the shingulls that pooped on it each day.

You Know What ... ?

Whitney Blair, a self-styled expert on seagulls and their propensity to deface signs, shared this crucial information with us:

"Many shingulls attack the same signs over and over again, seemingly holding a grudge against the sign or the owner for some reason. Some owners put French fries, bread crumbs, or even some plastic rodents outside to try to deter this activity, but these measures are usually ineffective. One legendary shingull was a large, black-backed gull named Oscar, who lived to be seventeen—great longevity for the species. Oscar claimed to have pooped on fifteen hundred lawyers' shingles and thirty-three hundred doctors' signs in his long, illustrious career."

Shirley Cue

Shirley Cue (n)—a pinkish pool stick designed especially for a female player

Sample Sentence: Big Bad Brendan almost got laughed out of the biker bar when he broke out his Shirley Cue, but the crowd went crying in their beer after he won all their money.

You Know What ... ?

The Shirley Cue was named for infamous pool hustler Shirley "Shnooker" Maloney, who earned a great living throughout the U.S. Midwest in the 1940s. Shirley frequented some seedy pool halls, accompanied by her manager and boyfriend, Arnie Wassle. Shnooker would usually lose a couple of games intentionally to Arnie, but she always got the guys' attention with her long legs and brash challenges to those on the neighboring tables.

Once the challenge was accepted, Ms. Maloney would return the house stick, take out her pink model, and proceed to win a ton of loot from the stunned gentlemen—employing her deadly combo of sex appeal and nine-ball expertise.

Shockwurst

Shockwurst (n)—a short, thick plastic sausage that has a low electric current running through it. This novelty piece is often favored by prop comics, conventioneers, and other wiseacres.

Sample Scenario: Ralph and Ed were good buddies who had met years back at an amateur magician's convention. They ran into each other every year at the Grand Rapids Showcase, where Ed would habitually shake Ralph's hand with an electric buzzer or shockwurst concealed in his palm. After falling for these tricks countless times, Ralph finally lost his temper and bashed Ed over the head with his toy gun.

Observation:

My friend (the Amazing) Rudy faxed me a list of his seven favorite props—other than the shockwurst:

- Cups and balls set
- Invisible grappler
- Floating handkerchiefs
- Magic coins
- Interlocking ring set
- Trick coloring books
- Self-immolating rabbit

Shoelice

Shoelice (n)—a wingless, parasitic insect that gravitates towards people's footwear

Please Note: The plural of shoelice is shoelice, not *shoelices*.

Sample Sentence: Sick and tired of the great proliferation of shoelice in the area that summer, (and hating loafers and sandals) Monica vowed to walk barefoot for the rest of her life.

Mastering the Word

There are five different types of lice that are parasitic to humans, according to Lila Washington, head researcher for the Leather and Lice Parasite Academy. Per Lila, "Many scientists categorize them as either sucking lice or chewing lice, but to me they all suck." The five types of lice are:

- Body lice
- Head lice
- Poetic lice
- Pubic lice
- Shoelice

Shoperatic

Shoperatic (adj)—reflecting an overly dramatic attitude towards shopping

Sample Sentence: Edgar was so shoperatic about his few excursions to the supermarket that his wife nicknamed him "The Shopper of Seville."

You Know What … ?

When I asked Dr. Marta Hari if shopaholics and shoperatic people are one and the same, she looked at me as if I had sprouted a fourth nostril. "What are you talking about, Matt? A shopaholic is addicted to shopping but isn't necessarily overly dramatic about it. She (or he) may be quite businesslike and even fatalistic.

"The shoperatic shopper usually acts all melodramatic because he/she doesn't go shopping very often. Got it?"

"So they are not mutually exclusive?" I countered.

"That's right, Matt," she added condescendingly.

Shortshoreman

Shortshoreman (n)—a diminutive person who works on the docks loading or unloading vessels

Please Note: In good-natured banter among dock workers of any size, longshoremen sometimes use it to describe those who unload small vessels. They are known to tease each other about their small workloads.

You Know What ... ?

Per the true shortshoremen, many had trouble breaking into the rough-and-tumble longshoremen unions (a very tough bunch affiliated with the AFL-CIO), and found that they had more power creating their own association. After going down to the docks several days in a row and not being chosen to work, itinerant worker Paolo "Pinky" Pinkarusso decided to take action.

In 1947, he organized a group—known as Pinky's Posse—that eventually became the International Shortshoreman Association. The ISA's original motto was, "We may be tiny, but we lift and curse like big, drunken stevedores." Ironically, or fittingly, they have had a long run and still exist today—thanks in no small part to Russo's efforts.

Skincipal

Skincipal (n)—the director or headmaster/ headmistress of a school that is part of a nudist colony

You Know What ... ?

You would think that skincipals would be chosen because of their good looks, but that is only partially true. In a 2007 survey conducted by *Buff Educators Weekly*, both students and teachers of nudist colonies were recently polled to ascertain, "What are the qualities you admire most in a good skincipal?"

Below were the qualities mentioned, from most to least important:

- Solid, but fair, discipline
- Innovative, with high academic standards
- Valuing the students' and teachers' individuality
- Lack of body hair (women) and rashes (men)
- Encouraging team sports
- Honoring the school's "Formal Friday" dress code (generally, bowties for men and high heels for ladies)
- Enforcing zero flatulence policies

Slaughty

Slaughty (adj)—a person (okay, a woman) who combines slatternly behavior with a lot of arrogance

You Know What ... ?

Blake Stucko owns and operates Class Act Escort Services, whose motto is "We may not get you the girl next door, but we can get you the one on the corner of your street." Catchy! Here's some more of Blake's wisdom:

"Guys always say that they value intelligence, a great sense of humor, love of family, and all that, but I figure that most men are really like me. They want to have a good time with a woman who is good-looking, lots of fun, and just this side of attainable. Well, we attain and retain some special women here at Class Act.

"One of our other sayings is, 'Our ladies are haughty, slaughty, and naughty.'"

When I asked Blake if it's true that these women won't leave clients feeling *distraughty*, he sounded impressed.

Slumbersome

Slumbersome (adj)—pertaining to box springs and mattresses (and the like) that are very unwieldy

Sample Scenario: When I asked Doug to help me move, he seemed kind of annoyed. "You never help me move," he replied. "But you've never moved, or moved anything heavy into your place since I've known you," I countered.

Doug thought for a moment and then replied, "Well, I'm still not helping you move those slumbersome mattresses you have."

You Know What ... ?

Research on "slumbersome mattresses" on the Net reveals what appears to be an urban legend indicating that mattresses double their weight due to all the dust mites and debris that enter into them. I have found no corroboration for this, and if you're thinking about buying that $2,000 super-duper vacuum cleaner that sucks out all the crap that you breathe in overnight, don't blame this book.

Slummerbund

Slummerbund (n)—a derogatory name given to describe a very cheaply made tuxedo

    b) the name given to a finely made tuxedo purchased at a cheap price.

Observation:

Like the word "cheap," this word is double-edged, as value is a very subjective thing to begin with. So which is the primary meaning? I don't know; usage seems to be split pretty evenly.

Sample Sentences:

A—Sensitive Sam refused to go to the senior prom with Heidi, who kept teasing him about the slummerbund he was wearing.

B—Although he had only worn a tuxedo twice in his life, the price to buy a slummerbund at Cheapo's Formal Wear was so low that Bruce couldn't pass one up.

Smacked Bass

Smacked Bass (n)—a certain type of game fish that tastes better after it's been smacked around for a few minutes

b) a person who incessantly extols the virtue of eating stripers

Sample Scenario: Rhonda was enjoying her blind dinner date with Jerry, who was pretty good company and was not bad-looking. That all changed when he ordered the striped bass and she went with the crab cakes. For the rest of the evening, the smacked bass kept criticizing her choice while bragging about how good and healthful his was.

You Know What ... ?

Chef Lucy LaRoo gives a quick tip for cooking smacked bass. "The key is, no matter how you garnish your bass—with garlic, scallions, lemon, cheese, mayo, whatever—you want to beat the living daylights out of it before broiling, baking, or frying it. Always remember that a beaten bass shows its gratitude with good flavor."

I never knew that.

Smellicose

Smellicose (adj)—descriptive of someone who stinks to high heaven *and* is very belligerent

Sample Scenario: When I met June at the airport, I couldn't help but notice her haggard appearance. Her explanation: "I knew I should've flown business class. In coach, I shared a transatlantic flight with the most smellicose man I have ever seen."

You Know What ... ?

Slippery Slope College commissioned a study to see if there is a strong correlation, little or no correlation, or even a negative correlation between smelling and acting offensively. Noxious odors professor Will Barnshaw oversaw the project and explained the results to me.

"The data was somewhat inconclusive. Unfortunately, that means we have to repeat the same experiment next fall. Time to round up all the miscreants, idiots, and smelly people along with blindfolds, survey forms, and industrial-strength fans. I think that only a small percentage of people are truly smellicose, but we'll see what happens in round two."

Snack-o-Lantern

Snack-o-Lantern (n)—an edible plastic pumpkin-shaped device with openings cut to represent the human eyes, nose, and mouth that are illuminated by a candle or other light

Observation:

Snack-o-lanterns became quite popular in the last few years, when families got tired of reusing their inedible jack-o-lanterns year after year. Although the edible plastic makes them more expensive, it has been found that users gladly pay more for the novelty of having an extra snack on hand.

Warning:

Would-be snack-o-lantern eaters should take care to remove the inedible candle before chomping away. There are approximately four hundred accidents related to neglecting this key step every year in New Jersey alone, and if we can prevent just one, this book has been well worth the effort.

Snobinson Crusoe

Snobinson Crusoe (n)—a derogatory term for a boy who is so conceited that he lives (at least figuratively) on his own island

Please Note: The term *Swiss Family Snobinson* was considered as an entry but alas was turned down by my editors. Not sure why; maybe, they didn't want to offend (or encourage?) our legions of Swiss readers.

Sample Sentence: When Imelda asked her son, Timmy, how his first day of high school was, he replied, "There are a bunch of weirdos there, which is okay, but I can't deal with all of the Snobinson Crusoes running around."

Mastering the Word

The classic novel *Robinson Crusoe* was authored by whom, and in which year?"

- a) Daniel Defore—1816
- b) Daniel Defore—Before 1816
- c) Daniel Defoe—1719
- d) Baniel Before—Before 1820
- e) Daniel Defoe—1819
- f) None of the above, but all are close.

Snorganic

Snorganic or Snoreganic (adj)—of, or related to, noisy sounds made overnight without the benefit of performance-enhancing drugs

Snorganic Chemistry (n)—the (new) study of how people who make strange nocturnal noises are attracted to one another

You Know What ... ?

Dr. Meg A. Hertz of Slippery Slope College led one of the nation's first snorganic chemistry research teams. I had the honor of interviewing her.

Matt: Meg, you headed an exciting snorganic chemistry research project in 2009. Will you tell us about it?

Dr. Hertz: Please call me Dr. Hertz.

Matt: Dr. Hertz, will you tell us about the project?

Dr. Hertz: Certainly. We matched young ladies from our sleep studies with young men from our campus dating board to study how well various snorers got along with one another.

Matt: Were there any problems with this interdisciplinary approach?

Dr. Hertz: Empirically? No. We got great data. Ethically? Maybe. Some of the gay and lesbian students protested that they were profiled out of the study.

Matt: That complaint aside, what were the results of your work?

Dr. Hertz: Due to the courageous work of my team, we came to these conclusions:

- Women who snored the loudest were most likely to be romantically involved with men who had less than perfect hearing. They did not do well with other loud snorers.
- Men suffering from periodic limb movement disorder did surprisingly well with women who had sleep apnea—but only if they flailed their legs when the women were awake.
- The loud snorers struck out with men who had rigid circadian rhythms, and vice-versa.
- The soft snorers, defined as never exceeding seventy-five decibels (dB), or about the sound level of a washing machine, did well with other soft snorers. This was especially true if the soft snorers were physically and sonically attracted to one another.

Pop Quiz

1. True or False: *Days of Swine and Noses* is *not* considered to be a great porcinema classic.

2. Gorging George Jefferson recommends that we eat cherry pie on Washington's Birthday in order to be more:
   a. penetrite
   b. pastriotic
   c. likely to visit a rodentist

3. Speaking of rodentists, what is Dr. Thorenson's favorite type of patient?

4. I mistook a piece of tofu for chicken. To my disgust, I bit into a:
   a. popsickle
   b. prolechariot
   c. misconstrudel

5. Lefty Crenshaw was considered the scourge of Silver City because of:
   a. his pinochle sandwiches
   b. his prowess with the Shirley cue
   c. his great card play
   d. his marksmanship

6. True or False: A cannabus is a great place to get high while traveling.

7. Dave Bresnahan was a minor league baseball player best known for his:
   a. retrosexual behavior
   b. hit-and-shun expertise
   c. vivid imashination
   d. graceful pirouwets

8. Pumperdimes and bilkshakes share this characteristic:
   a. They are both means of transportation.
   b. Both are overpriced.
   c. They are both types of shingulls.

9. How many American doctors have been accused of chiromania in the last decade?
   a. Millions
   b. None
   c. more than 1,200

10. Which of these *is not* a famous prognocrastination of Harry Honto?
   a. This book will sell millions.
   b. Dewey defeats Truman.
   c. Mets win the 1969 World Series.
   d. "W" will butcher the English language.

FROM SPAMURAI TO ZOO-CHINI

Spamurai

Spamurai (n)—a person descended from Japanese feudal warriors who disrupts others' e-mail or Internet usage

Please Note: *Spamurai* has come to mean any disruptive electronic message sent by someone from Japan.

Observation:

One day, while surfing the net from a local library, I grew frustrated by all the spam that was interrupting my usage. "Damn, this spamurai sucks," I inadvertently shouted out loud. Little did I know that my Japanese friend, Mieko, overheard me. She rebuked me, saying "How do you know it came from Japan? It could have come from India, or Canada, or Europe, or the United States, or from someone right next door. How do you know? What makes you so sure?"

When I tried to explain that the message had Japanese characters, it didn't help. "How do *you* know? How do you *know*? Just because there's Japanese writing, it does not mean it came from there. It could have been fake spamurai."

I have to admit that Mieko made some fine points.

Spermodynamic

Spermodynamic (adj)—very potent; capable of fathering multiple children

Sample Sentence: Russ, a father of thirteen, was extremely proud of his yellow T-shirt that proclaimed, *Spermodynamic Stud* in bold red letters.

You Know What ... ?

The Web site www.infoplease.com displays an interesting chart showing that the average size of an American household (by number of people—not by the weight of each person) has been declining steadily over the years, from a high of almost 5 per household in 1890 to a low of about 2.5 today. Is this a matter of reduced spermodynamics? Possibly so, but it is probably attributable to many other factors, such as the greater range of reproductive options today and the higher number of single-parent households.

The data shows that in 2006, the average size of a "married couple family" household is 3.210, and the average size of a "living alone" household is 1.000, whether male or female. I would have guessed the latter statistic, though it's good to see it in print.

Spinal Tapioca

Spinal Tapioca (n)—a pudding given to patients to calm them down after their spinal cords have been punctured

Sample Sentence: Susie dreaded going to the hospital for her invasive procedure, but the spinal tapioca seemed to make it all worthwhile.

Observation:

Cheryl Bitman, head of Our Lady of Mediocre Health's excellent Post-Surgery Cuisine Department, lists the preferred food items given to patients after various procedures:

- **Breast Reduction Surgery**—Chicken (a small amount of white meat) with parsley potatoes
- **Gastric Bypass**—Beef burritos with chili
- **Hip Replacement**—Cereal, skim milk, and fruit
- **Hernia Repair**—Something light
- **Knee Replacement**—Fish sticks and sauerkraut
- **Laser Vision Correction**—Peas, carrots, and candy
- **Lobotamies**—Split pea soup with a side of pasta
- **Open Heart**—*Lefties* from hernia repair
- **Rhinoplasty**—Limburger cheese and garlic donuts

Squashbuckler

Squashbuckler (n)—someone who devours food of the gourd family with a certain swagger

Please Note: *Squashbuckler* may be applied to suave eaters of corn, peas, and carrots. It can also be used to describe a movie that features the showy eating of these vegetables.

Sample Scenario: Before I went out to dinner with Guillermo, I knew he was kind of cocky. But even in my wildest dreams, I could not imagine that he was a genuine squashbuckler.

Observation:

Miley Tortelli, a Hollywood historian, noted that while famous, swashbuckling actors such as Tyrone Power, Basil Rathbone, and Douglas Fairbanks all ate their meals with excellent manners, Errol Flynn was known as "the pirate of the commissary." Per Ms. Tortelli, Flynn would regularly take an overgrown squash, cut it into small pieces with his sword, and yell, "Ahoy, mates," before eating each little piece.

Stegoscope

Stegoscope (n)—device used to check the heartbeat of extinct animals

Please Note: *Stegoscope* (along with its adjectival form, *stegoscopic*) has evolved to connote almost anything of very questionable value.

Sample Sentence: Monica was furious with Joe after he described the mittens she sewed for her poodle as stegoscopic.

You Know What ... ?

Enter Professor Ava Lubnick, head of Slippery Slope's prestigious Paleontology Department:

"The stegoscope, of course, originated when certain dinosaur fanatics refused to believe that their beloved creatures were truly dead. Their unofficial leader was a diehard scientist named Nigel Stuffel, who famously traveled from Croydon, England, to Laramie, Wyoming, to listen to the heartbeat of the juvenile fossil remains of a stegosaurus. A BBC film crew covered this event, and the name stegoscope (more catchy than *Stuffelscope*) stuck."

Stupometer

Stupometer (n)—an electronic device that measures the stupidity of someone or something, flashing red flags and sounding alarms that are invisible and inaudible to the nonuser

Sample Sentence: Whenever I attend one of my weekly sales seminars, my stupometer is so active that I have trouble concentrating.

You Know What ... ?

Here are a few fun facts about stupometers:

- While the first models weighed 120 pounds and cost $1,000 or more, there are now excellent pocket models that cost $12.99 or less.
- Bowing to pressure from teachers' unions, stupometers are forbidden in many school districts.
- Unofficially, the highest known stupometer readings have occurred at Pauly Shore stand-up comedy performances and films, *Jerry Springer Show* tapings, and Tea Party conventions.

Suckulent

Suckulent (adj)—descriptive of any food that tastes good at first but then has a hideous aftertaste

Observation:

My friend Lynn is a wonderful person who prides herself on her cooking. Indeed, some of her meals are quite good. Yet, some of her dishes are so suckulent that I can only stay a few minutes after dinner before having to excuse myself.

You Know What ... ?

Lars McKinney had an excellent piece in the August 2009 edition of *Belcher's Digest*, which I am sampling with his permission:

"Many diners—whether public belchers or not—have complained to me that some of their favorite foods have a suckulent effect on them. Everything from pot roast to corn on the cob to black bean dishes leaves a bad taste in their mouth—and in their memories. My advice: Consider the aftertaste as well as the taste in choosing foods. Don't be short-sighted; evaluate food with all of your senses and premonitions."

Suemommy

Suemommy (n)—unofficial name given to a class of frivolous lawsuits filed by children against their parents

Sample Scenario: Family law attorney Horace Gallagher was upset about the lack of quality cases he had been receiving. "All I get is uncontested divorces and some stinking suemommies," he groused.

You Know What ... ?

Top six (typical) complaints in a suemommy are:

- Not enough TV time
- Lack of breast milk stunted growth
- Refused to help with homework
- Embarrassment at Little League games
- Allowances received were less than the median for their hometown
- Other siblings, and even neighbors' pets, were hugged and kissed more often

Tae-Cant-Do

Tae-Cant-Do (n)—a Jewish-Korean form of martial arts that died out because the moves invented by the master were considered to be too impossible to duplicate

You Know What ... ?

The discipline—invented in 1938 by the mysterious Hyman Creamshee Lee—combined unique elements of karate, self-defense, prayer, chutzpah, and noshing. Said Lee, "Tae-Cant-Do is the nexus of greed, unselfishness, flexibility, ego, hunger, privation, and supplication. Don't try this at home."

Observation:

Tae-Cant-Do has come to describe any assignment that is impossible to execute. An alternative, accepted form of the word is *Me-Cant-Do.*

Sample Sentence: I told Professor Cumberbatch that writing a thirty-page term paper overnight would be an exercise in Tae-Cant-Do.

Talibanjo

Talibanjo (n)—a stringed instrument manufactured in Afghanistan most often played by Islamic fundamentalists

Sample Sentence: Even though I had no use for Mullah's political doctrines, I had to admit that he played one mean Talibanjo.

You Know What ... ?

Members of the Taliban are often portrayed as joyless brutes subject to Sharia law and incapable of even enjoying music. "That is mostly true," offered Afghan/Italian scholar Mohammed Al-Valentino, "but the musical allegation is false. Many followers of this movement enjoy playing the Talibanjo, which combines traditional Islamic music with American bluegrass."

Al-Valentino mentioned that some of the most popular Talibanjo music even plays off American rock and roll standards. According to the scholar, ten of the most popular Talibanjo songs are:

- "Rebel, Rebel, Your Face Has No Beard"
- "You Bin Laden on My Mind"
- "We'll Be Surging up the Mountain"
- "Islama-Bad Girls"
- "Skip to Mu-llah, My Darling"
- "My Sharia More"
- "The Ballad of Amir Clampett"
- "Al Qaeda River for You"
- "Kabuli Waltz"
- "Dueling Talibanjoes"

Tallis Man

Tallis Man (n)—a very diminutive employee of some synagogues who is in charge of giving everyone their lucky prayer shawl (tallis) before the start of the service

Sample Sentence: Chaim was so cute, and such a good tallis man, that Mordechai wanted to wear him around his neck for good luck.

Please Note: For better or for worse, this practice has become almost obsolete. Shortly, there will be no more tallis men.

You Know What … ?

Milton Milkstein, Executive Director of the Little Jewish People Anti-Discrimination League, shared this with us: "Thankfully, the tallis man is becoming a thing of the past. Three of my ancestors held this position, but this was less about prestige than it was about getting any work at all.

The job was frequently difficult, and many tallis men still suffer from carpal tunnel syndrome because of all of the folding and unfolding of the prayer shawls."

Tattle Call

Tattle Call (n)—an open interview where a company looks to hire the biggest snitch(es) in a room full of applicants

Sample Sentence: After having my trust betrayed yet again by Donny, I suggested that he check the listings to see if there were any tattle calls in the area.

You Know What ... ?

"Hiring a good company snitch is tricky business, and more and more companies are turning to smaller specialists like us," noted Mario Robustelli, CEO of A Snitch in Time Recruiting. "We often hold tattle calls, which are more time-efficient than one-on-one interviews."

So what qualities is Mario looking for? "Inquisitive people—those who are nosey and can provide inside information. A former mobster gone informant is always good, as is any other criminal informant. Most of all, we value ambitious people who would betray their own family, friends, and associates for an opportunity to get ahead."

Televisionary

Televisionary (n)—one who has the power to see what will be shown next on television

Observation:

Watching TV with a televisionary is not usually a good thing. I have had a few friends who have fit this description, and they would spoil the suspense of any program that we were watching.

The role of a televisionary has changed over the years. In the so-called golden era of television— long before the advent of on-screen programming menus—a televisionary was someone who could predict what show was coming on next. The better ones could even foresee what was going to happen next within a particular show.

Nowadays, a true televisionary can predict—with 95 percent accuracy or higher—everything from the final score of a game to lines of dialogue in a sitcom to the denouement of a thriller. That being said, if you suspect that someone you're watching a game or movie with is a televisionary, I recommend that you either kick him/her out or shut off the tube. You'll thank me later for my sage advice.

Thunderstore

Thunderstore (n)—a retail establishment that only sells rain-related items

Please Note: While not popular in places like Phoenix or LA, thunderstores came into vogue recently in Seattle and in other cities that frequently resemble rain forests.

Sample Sentence: Complaining that she had nothing to keep her feet dry, I told Rebecca that I would drive her over to the thunderstore, where they had a sale on galoshes.

You Know What ... ?

Esoteric Retail Magazine listed the top six American thunderstore chains in 2009:

1. Osh Kosh Galosh
2. Wet-Smart
3. Umbrella City
4. How Dry R Us
5. Fleece Me Dry
6. Wet Blankets

Tiaromatic

Tiaromatic (adj)—smelling like a beauty queen, this term is often used sarcastically

Sample Sentence: Rebecca Fogle was the envy of many of her classmates for her straight *A*s, perfect looks, and tiaromatic scent.

You Know What ... ?

Dr. Marta Hari has some strong opinions on this word: "I was a beauty queen during my school days, and I aroused jealousy and other feelings in my peers. Girls wanted to be like me, and boys wanted to date me. A few lucky ones did—each and every semester. That aside, I always wanted to smell like a beauty queen—even in gym class—and I'm not so sure what's wrong with that. The green-eyed monster of jealousy was always trained on me; I just didn't let it devour me.

"My so-called friends would accuse me of trying extra hard to smell tiaromatic. Should I have smelled like a fellow barnyard animal after gym class just to assuage their self-esteem? I don't play that."

Tirish

Tirish (n)—the English language as spoken by very tired people. Some of the Asian and Arabic countries appear to also have derivatives of this language, and Tirish is beginning to be taught overseas at many secondary schools as an elective.

Sample Sentence: While I strained to hear everything my beloved wife uttered, the Tirish she spoke was unintelligible.

You Know What ... ?

Enter Frieda Wilmont, head of Slippery Slope College's Unusual Languages Department. "Tirish is one of the leading languages of the future. I would estimate that 98 percent of all Americans speak it at one time or another, and almost everything under the sun is spoken about in Tirish. Our students learn important phrases such as *Wama vulla loo*—which, depending on the inflection, could mean any of the following:

- Can you hand me the remote?
- Please set my alarm clock for 7:30.
- Wow! The Eagles won again?!
- Any food in the fridge?
- We need more troops in Afghanistan."

Tonsilation

Tonsilation (n)—the act of offering a prominent oval mass of lymphoid tissue removed from the throat to cheer someone up

Sample Sentence: After all the years I had been friends with Gemma, I thought it fitting to offer her tonsilation after her pet raccoon died suddenly.

You Know What ... ?

Dick Driscoll, the CEO of Lost Companions, a pet cemetery in Wheeling, West Virginia, spoke to us about this practice. "While you or I may appreciate receiving someone's lymphoid tissue after our family pet dies, I'm not so sure this is the proper thing to give to others in their time of grief. Unless I know the recipient is open to tonsilation, I would look to console him in other ways." Driscoll prefers the following, more traditional expressions of sympathy.

- Flowers
- A card—sentimental poem optional
- A favorite picture of the pooch, cat, etc.
- A gift card, but not to a pet store
- Gift certificate to a nearby buffet

Touchup

Touchup (n)—in football, the opposite of a touchdown, when a player mistakenly runs the wrong way and scores points (technically two points for a safety) for the opposing team

Sample Scenario: I still remember the touchup I scored in a middle school flag football game. I spun around to intercept a pass and then streaked untouched to the end zone and spiked the ball. Little did I know that I had scored two points for the other team and would be nicknamed "Goalpost Goldberg" for the next year or so.

Observation:

There were two very famous misdirected runs in football history—one in the NFL by Minnesota Vikings great Jim Marshall and one in college football by California's Roy "Wrong Way" Riegels.

In 1964, Marshall scooped up a fumble, spun around, and ran sixty-six yards to the wrong end zone and threw the ball out of play, inadvertently scoring two points for the San Francisco 49ers. The Vikings did recover to win the game 27–22. Marshall also recovered to have a storied career as a nineteen-year member of the Vikings. He was a fixture on the defensive line of a great Vikings defense (led by Hall of Famers Alan Page and Carl Eller) that was known as "the Purple People Eaters." Until his record was broken very recently by Brett Favre, Marshall had started in 270 straight NFL games.

The even more infamous touchup (although, technically, it was not that) was committed by Riegels, a University of California Bears two-way lineman who would make All-America the following year. Playing in the 1929 Rose Bowl against Georgia Tech, Riegels recovered a fumble and pivoted the wrong way, starting for what he thought would be six points for his team. He made it sixty-five yards until a teammate caught up to him and pointed him in the right direction. Unfortunately, three

Georgia Tech players arrived and tackled him on his own one-yard line. Rather than risk a safety on the next play, Cal decided to punt, but you guessed it—Tech blocked it and scored a safety for a 2–0 lead. Cal would end up scoring, and Riegels would even re-enter the game and block a punt himself, but Tech beat Cal to win the Rose Bowl by a score of 8–7.

Riegels, who went on to great success in and out of sports, was always known by this one blunder—and it was not even a touchup—just a little #$@!-*up*.

Treevial

Treevial (adj)—possessing an exhaustive (and exhausting) amount of knowledge about trees

Please Note: A synonym for *treevial* that some prefer is *arbore-real*. *Treeviality* and *arbore-reality* are equally valid word forms.

Sample Sentence: Jack annoys me every single time with his need to share every treevial fact and figure with me.

Observation:

Curiously, with all of the television networks available, there have been very few (if any) arbore-reality TV series. Not that there would be too many people pining away for such a show.

If there *are* any networks that are looking for some treevial new shows, I propose the following series titles:

- *This Old Tree*
- *More and More Sycamores*
- *Sap Me Quickly*
- *Making an Ash Out of Myself*

Trombonus

Trombonus (n)—extra remuneration received in exchange for the skillful playing of a brass instrument

Sample Sentence: "I'm going to switch to the clarinet," said Petra, an angry professional musician who never received her trombonus from the orchestra.

Mastering the Word

A *trombonus* only relates to extra money paid to players of brass instruments. Believe it or not, all but one of the following musical instruments are considered to be brass. Can you find the errant one?

- euphonium
- fat trumpet
- flumpet
- kakaki
- sackbut
- strumpet
- superbone

Big Hint: A strumpet might have played a superbone at one time or another.

Try-cycle

Try-cycle (n)—an extremely slow moving four-wheeled vehicle, pedaled by very young children and older, more cautious adults

Sample Sentence: Alfie was advised by his usually overprotective mom to leave his try-cycle at home and get up the courage to bring a tricycle or bicycle with him to college.

You Know What ... ?

Dennis Marsh, proprietor of the Philadelphia store Trikes For Tykes, is an expert on try-cycles. Per Marsh, "We generally recommend the try-cycle for those not yet ready for the dangers of a tricycle or for the perils of a bicycle with training wheels. Because it has four wheels, the try-cycle is very sturdy. It's designed to go no more than half a mile per hour, yet we have some exciting designs that help to remove the stigma for the older try-cycle peddler.

In addition to the sleek designs, we sponsor try-cycle races in four age groups: 2; 3–4; 5–6, and 7–107."

Turtle-itarian

Turtle-itarian (adj)—pertaining to a government run by a very slow-moving autocrat

Please Note: As I understand the term, in a turtle-itarian regime, the wheels of justice (or injustice) don't necessarily move slowly—the dictator himself does. Hopefully, my discussion with Steve Doglin will clarify this.

Matt: Steve, in your new book, *Corpulent Despots,* you define "turtle-itarian" as something resembling an authoritarian government run by a very slow-moving dictator. Is that accurate?

Steve: Pretty close. But remember, "turtle-itarian" does not only apply to a country's government. It could also describe any organization that is run with an iron fist—one that represses any dissent from its constituents or members. And the dictator of this body must, personally, be a very slow mover.

Matt: Sticking to governmental regimes that we may know, were any of the following governments—those run by Mussolini, Hitler, or Stalin—considered to be turtle-itarian?

Steve: You mentioned some horrible despots, but all moved too quickly to have this status. Famous turtle-itarian leaders would include Uganda's infamous Idi Amin, who had an athletic background but became fat and slow. There's Mao Zedong. While he propagated China's so-called Great Leap Forward, he himself inched along like a wounded snail.

And in his later years, Cambodia's horrific Pol Pot would qualify. Pol Pot was known to sit on his toilet for hours at a time. An impertinent staffer once knocked on his bathroom door and yelled at him to "piss or get off the pot." The Khmer Rouge leader did not have much of a sense of humor. He had three of his henchmen remove the staffer's belly button with pliers, hang him upside down, and skin him alive.

Matt: Thanks for that beautiful word picture, Steve. Now, in terms of nongovernmental leaders, who might be considered turtle-itarian?

Steve: Anyone and everyone from your school board president to the commissioner of, well, a men's softball league.

Matt: A men's softball league?! I can't imagine that a recreational league for over-the-hill ballplayers could be ruled by an iron-fisted monarch who moves at a glacial pace.

Steve: You had better believe it. Didn't you read the case example I provided in the last chapter of my book?

Matt: No, I haven't read that far yet.

Steve: Well, read it! It goes into the ways the league's commissioner must restore order to his league by quelling dissent—all in the best interests of all teams and members.

Matt: I didn't realize that running a league was fraught with such dangers. Maybe I should—

Steve: Read it! Read it now!

Matt: Are you the commissioner in question, or is the case study about someone else you know, or someone you invented?

Steve: Are you challenging my veracity and authority? *Read* it. *Read the stinking chapter!*

Matt: Okay. Okay. Are you bullying me?

Steve: Just kidding. I thought you, of all people, would have a sense of humor. Guess not.

Tweetise

Tweetise (n)—a 140-character (or fewer) paper that purports to be scholarly

Sample Sentence: Although restricted by the guidelines of her favorite Web site, Lana labored hard to impress the other members of her faculty with her daily tweetises.

Rant:

I'm sure that more than half the known universe now knows about Twitter, which encourages us to post and reply instantaneously about anything and everything. Are we such a self-important and self-promoting society that we have to "tweet" every single time we go to the movies, buy a loaf of bread, or scratch our navel? Can we only speak in little 140-character missives? Do we really need to reassure ourselves by accumulating so-called followers, friends, and people who are linked to us? Do we need to speak with cool abbreviations and shopworn emoticons?

Let me re-tweet this:

just scratched my butt when buying bread. 2 kewl, lol, saw M Moore film 2day—6.5–back later, lol, need more tweeps 2 follow me—ttfn, lol.

Unicyclops

Unicyclops (n)—in Greek mythology, a huge, one-eyed beast who enjoyed riding a one-wheeler. Many of them were able to juggle.

You Know What ... ?

Euripides Amenides, professor of classic literature at Slippery Slope College, said that the unicyclops was, generally, a very friendly creature. "There were said to be about a hundred unicyclopes (the preferred plural form) who lived in Ancient Greece, and the average adult stood thirty feet tall, weighed 988 pounds, and rode the unicycle with reckless abandon. They loved children and would wink merrily at them—albeit with one huge eye that was in the middle of their forehead. Tragically, the wink petrified many children, and would-be romantic partners as well.

"Very, very few people befriended the unicyclops, and that's also a shame. There were no good optometrists to serve them and not enough circuses and weddings for them to sustain a living. They just kind of died out."

Vegestarian

Vegestarian (n)—one who is mesmerized by the appearance and aura of vegetables, often unnerving one's tablemates in the process

Sample Sentence: Ruthie vowed to never return to the vegestarian convention, allowing that she would feel more comfortable at a table of cannibals.

You Know What ... ?

One of the pleasures of writing this book is the opportunity to speak with fascinating people, such as Mars Greenman, author of the powerful, *Ogling Okra: My Life as a Vegestarian.* Below is part of our conversation:

Matt: Mars, how did you become a vegestarian?

Mars: My mom forced me to eat a lot of vegetables.

Matt: Is there more to the story? Your book's 455 pages long.

Mars: There is, but I find it easier to write about than to talk about. It's very painful, but I'll try. We were forced—sometimes at gunpoint—to clean our plates before we were allowed to leave the dinner table. My sister, Lana, had no problems with this policy and went on to become a competitive broccoli-eating champion.

Matt: Didn't know there was such a thing.

Mars: Oh, yes. She's the world champ. But I just could not stomach all of the root vegetables, lima beans, okra, broccoli, and Brussels sprouts ... what am I forgetting ... that we were forced to eat. So I would try to wait out my parents by staring at my plate till they would eventually give up and let me either give them to my sister or throw them down the drain.

Matt: Did you do the same with the other food groups—your meats, poultry, fruits, bre—

Mars: No, no problem with any of those. I'm not a carnistarian or an omnistarian.

Matt: Hmmm. I didn't know there were such people.

Mars: There should be, but I guess the words aren't catchy enough.

Matt: Vegetable juices. Any problems?

Mars: Nope.

Matt: What problems has being a vegestarian caused for you?

Mars: I got laughed at in school cafeterias and was frequently late going to my next class. Eating out on dates, or even with friends, became traumatic experiences. You know, we have a society that forgives thieves, rapists, murderers, and politicians, but the minute you start counting peas and analyzing the color of rutabagas, you're a freak. A pariah. An outcast. A m—

Matt: I think I get the picture. How many vegestarians are there in the United States, and are there support groups?

Mars: It is estimated that there are about twenty-seven of us, but I'm sure there are many more. That just counts the ones who are brave enough to go to the VA meetings.

Matt: Vegestarians Anonymous?

Mars: Yup.

Velcro-Magnon

Velcro-Magnon (n)—Upper Paleolithic forerunners of homo sapiens who had long heads, broad faces, deep-set eyes, and the almost pathological need to stick together in caves and huts

Sample Sentence: My quick-witted niece, Elyse, describes some of the dumb jocks who always stick together at school as Velcro-Magnon.

Observation:

In reading about the Velcro-Magnon, a few items stood out:

- They were essentially modern for their time, spoke French quite well, and had mastered at least one other language passably well.
- As modern beings, they were quite skilled at making clothing and wore the finest labels (but alas, Velcro wasn't invented for another seventeen thousand or so years).
- They seemed to have lived between thirty thousand and seventeen thousand years ago, although efforts to date their fossils have proven to be frustrating, uneventful, and downright distasteful!

Web Trousers

Web Trousers (n)—the name given to special pants worn when surfing the Internet

Sample Sentence: Professor Paxson never researched anything online without first changing into his favorite pair of Web trousers.

You Know What ... ?

I spend a huge amount of time at my PC each day but have never really thought about what to wear. I asked my friend, Bev Glooky, owner of Virtual Pants, for advice about the type of trousers I should be wearing while surfing the Web.

- Jeans—"Good for everyday needs, but they don't facilitate serious research."
- Corduroys—"Too restrictive. I only recommend them for the occasional e-mail."
- Dress pants—"Nah, not versatile enough, and they don't encourage long sessions."
- Sweat pants—"Not a bad choice, but my first choice would be—"
- Underwear—"Whether boxers or briefs (and I'm a brief girl), they let you be you and save you money at the same time."

Wevelwee

Wevelwee (n)—the celebration of the inability to pronounce English correctly, usually on the part of native French speakers

Sample Sentence: Wishing to add to Pierre and Henri's sense of wevelwee at the fast food restaurant, I ordered them a special batch of Fwench fwies.

Observation:

I showed this entry to my Parisian friend, Francoise Lemieux, but she wasn't too happy about it. Here's a somewhat accurate transcript of the barrage she directed at me (and at all of you dear readers who are having an immature laugh at her expense).

"You must be quite pwoud of yousef, making fun of our pwonunciation. Weally, weally funny. As if you know the foost thing about Fwench. Fwench is ze number one Womance language, and your cwiticism of the lack of 'r' sound is widiculous. Zis is weally, weally ... um ... *quite* disgusting for you to wevel in your wibald humor and wevile us in such a wepugnant manner."

(I'd delete it, but it's already gone to "pwess.")

Whoreticulture

Whoreticulture (n)—the study of prostitutes, including an in-depth look at their diet, culture, and techniques

Sample Sentence: Up against the deadline for deciding upon a college major, Slacker Epstein decided that he would major in whoreticulture.

You Know What … ?

I spoke with Dr. Lisa Efstein, professor of whoreticulture at Slippery Slope College, about this exciting field of study.

Matt: Dr. Efstein, how long has whoreticulture been an academic option at Slippery Slope?

Dr E: It's been an official major for ten years, but whoreticulture has thrived on our beautiful campus for as long as I can remember.

Matt: Do more men or women major in whoreticulture?

Dr E: It used to be 95 percent men, some of whom signed up without realizing how rigorous our curriculum is. Now, it's about fifty/fifty.

Matt: What makes your curriculum so rigorous?

Dr E: Slippery Slope, as you must realize, has the highest academic standards. In such an institution, which values research, a typical whoreticulture class emphasizes a lot of independent research—which can be quite exhausting. Or so I've heard.

Matt: I would not think that would be a problem for men, but why are women signing up?

Dr E: There are some male escorts who come in as guest lecturers. Also, we have been able to set up quite a few very exciting internships with local establishments.

Matt: What can a student learn from studying the history of prostitution from around the globe?

Dr E: Besides learning about this important history, as human beings we are always curious about the past and inquisitive about other cultures. Some say that there is nothing new under the sun, and that you can't teach an old dog a new trick. Well, the *dogs* we teach are not that old, and I have taught most of them a new trick or two.

Wimpanzee

Wimpanzee (n)—a timid anthropoid ape of tropical Africa, noted for both its intelligence and cowardice

Sample Sentence: Little Johnny threw a peanut in the direction of a gang of wimpanzees, who all reacted as if he had detonated a nuclear bomb.

You Know What ... ?

Joan Badall, the noted African wimpanzee advocate, had this tidbit to pass along.

"The wimpanzee is the closest living relative to the human being, even though they split in their evolutionary development about 4.5 million years ago. They belong to the same family as us (Hominidae), and they sometimes attend the same family reunions, which can be remarkably large affairs.

"If inviting a wimpanzees to such a reunion, please remember to give them the star treatment with respect to travel accommodations and food. They are extremely sensitive and will cry if they are treated with a lack of respect and deference."

Wintersault

Wintersault (n)—a tumbling motion executed outdoors in extremely cold weather

Sample Sentence: With the gymnasium closed for inclement weather, Rachel turned some beautiful wintersaults in the snow.

You Know What ... ?

Outdoor gymnastics is not a well-known sport here, but it used to be quite popular in the former Soviet Union. A friend of mine told me about an unbelievable outdoor gymnast named Ludmilla Martin, whom I had the honor of interviewing. While speaking with her, I had to suppress the urge to say "wow" about a hundred times. Here's some of our conversation.

Matt: Ludmilla, you were once described as Russia's greatest ever outdoor gymnast. Is that true?

Ludmilla: I don't know, but I do know that I won every meaningful outdoor competition ever held in my country. Did you ever hear of Olga Korbut?

Matt: Yes. She was amazing.

Ludmilla: Okay, I beat the Little Flea every time we competed. She hated that nickname, by the way. Olga was four-foot-nothing, and I stood nearly 6′9″ tall—gargantuan for a gymnast—yet I was much more graceful.

Matt: So why didn't you compete in the 1972 Olympics, when Olga was winning all those gold medals?

Ludmilla: I hate indoor gymnastics! Real gymnasts compete in snow, ice, and wind, where it is more difficult. Indoors is for the faint of heart.

Matt: Do you resent the fame that she and some of the other Russian gymnasts have achieved?

Ludmilla: Resent? No, I stand by my decision. But I do hate Olga for stealing my boyfriend, Anatoly.

Matt: So why did such a, um, big lady like yourself gravitate toward gymnastics?

Ludmilla: Other sports were not a challenge. I averaged thirty-five points per game as the center for the Soviet Olympic basketball team. Hockey? I was a bone-crushing defenseman who dominated men. You ever hear of Vasily Alekseyev?

Matt: Yes. The legendary Olympic weightlifter?

Ludmilla: Okay. I defeated him in arm wrestling five years in a row. But gymnastics was my passion.

Matt: Did you have a favorite apparatus?

Ludmilla: I excelled in all of them, but I loved the balance beam. An official balance beam is only 10 centimeters wide, you know. Well, I petitioned our Wintersault Federation to narrow it to 8.5. That's all the room I needed to do my splits and back handsprings. They denied my petition. Is there anything else you'd like to know?

Matt: Ludmilla, your last name is unusual for a Russian athlete. Is your background mixed, like that of another great Russian gymnast, Nellie Kim, who was half-Korean?

Ludmilla: No, both my parents were born in Belarus, as were their parents. My maiden name is quite long—Gordeevaskayarenko. Almost as long as me. After I lost my Anatoly for good, I moved to the United States and married an American guy. I willingly gave up my maiden name, although the last names of my three boys are hyphenated.

Womandacious

Womandacious (adj)—dishonest; habitually prevaricating—in the way that (some) women often do. *Womandacious* is the female counterpart of **mandacious** (please see entry).

Sample Scenario: Shavonne was known to be a marvelous businesswoman who treated her employees and clientele quite well. She was also respected as a good wife, mother, and trusted friend. Having said all that, she could also be quite womandacious about topics she felt were nobody else's business.

You Know What … ?
According to a recent poll taken by *Wily Women Illustrated,* womandacious behavior often involves these five topics:
- true hair color
- age
- weight
- past relationships
- culinary ability

Wrathskeller

Wrathskeller (n)—a basement beer joint specially designed for angry patrons

Observation:

The first known wrathskeller was opened in Sweden, not Germany. This shocked me, as Swedes seem so mellow. But as my friend, Bjorn Henstrom, might say, "Maybe that's the reason why."

Today, many colleges and universities (yes, including Slippery Slope College) have a wrathskeller on campus that is often nicknamed "The Angry Rat."

Slippery Slope's captain of campus security, Brock Winger, told us, "You would think that wrathskellers would have a lot of violent disturbances, but that has not been my experience. In 2008, we made one hundred arrests on campus, and only eleven of them happened at 'The Angry Rat.' Contrast that number with sixteen in the dorms, twenty-eight in the library, and thirty-three at our faculty meetings."

Yellowcution

Yellowcution (n)—the ability to speak eloquently while waiting for the traffic light to turn green

Sample Sentence: Every time I ride in the car with Jose, I can't wait for the red lights to appear so I can sit back and marvel at his gift of yellowcution.

Please Note: Under unusually busy conditions, yellowcution may be employed at stop signs and blinking lights as well. When meteorological conditions are just right, **blink verse** (please see entry) may also be recited.

Observation:

I was startled to learn that my favorite institution of higher learning, Slippery Slope College, offered no classes in yellowcution. I discussed this with the admissions director, Phyllis Inonit, on the way to lunch. While waiting for a green light, I demonstrated to Phyllis that I could present quite a case for it, employing speed talking, thinking on my butt, etc.

Asked if she was impressed by my yellowcution, she retorted, "No, not really. While you were busy talking, you ignored the light changing nine times, eighteen cars honked at you, twelve ladies, including me, flipped you the bird, and we almost got rear-ended three times."

Yepidemic

Yepidemic (n)—a rapidly developing, widespread period of informal agreement between parties

Sample Sentence: The U.S. Congress actually passed a couple of bills during their short-lived yepidemic, but when that period passed, they reverted to their old partisan ways.

Please Note: When a roll call vote passes with at least a 95 percent majority, it is sometimes referred to as a yepidemic. Some prefer to spell this word "yupidemic," and that's okay by me.

Observation:

Wendi Branaugh is the author of a self-published book that recounts the details of every roll-call vote ever taken in the U.S. Senate. Entitled *Wake Me When It's My Turn,* the 12,865 page book can be ordered from www.adnauseumpress.com for only $500.

Ms. Branaugh notes that a senator once made a motion to adopt the following for their informal roll call votes: "yep" for *yea,* "nope" for *nay,* and "I'm outta here" for *not voting.* Unfortunately, it was tabled after a lengthy filibuster by a Republican junior senator from Idaho.

Yom Kippurim

Yom Kippurim (n)—a relatively new Jewish holiday that occurs around June 15. It combines fasting and solemn repentance with periods of unmitigated joy. While the fasting is done for most of the day, followers of this holiday are allowed one hamentashen, one glass of wine, and one zany circle dance—if done between 3:00 and 3:30 PM.

Sample Sentence: The officers of Congregation Sons of Doctors were gratified that their first-ever Yom Kippurim service drew more than a hundred members to the schul.

You Know What ... ?

I was surprised to hear that Renaissance Rabbi Gersh Lewin did not celebrate Yom Kippurim. He graciously met up with me for a short interview.

Matt: Hello, Rabbi Lewin.

Gersh: Please, it's Gersh.

Matt: Gersh, why do you oppose Yom Kippurim? Sounds like a good idea to me.

Gersh: Do Christians have an *Eastmas* combining Easter and Christmas?

Matt: I'm Jewish, and don't think so, but why do we need to follow others?

Gersh: Did I imply that we are followers? My point is that Purim is about pure joy, and Yom Kippur is about repentance, self-reflection, and self-improvement. How can I confess to God about my sins, or the sins of my community, if I am doing a drunken circle dance? Does it make sense to you?

Matt: I thought it did. Anything else to add on the subject?

Gersh: Do *you* have anything else to add?

Matt: I forget who was asking the questions here.

Gersh: Do you usually ask the questions? Don't you learn just as much when you answer questions? Don't you believe in the Socratic approach? Are you anti-Socratic?

Zoo-chini

Zoo-chini (n)—green summer squash served uniquely to animals in a zoo

Sample Sentence: I often go early to the animal park just so I have a chance to watch the baboons tear into some fresh zoo-chini.

You Know What ... ?

Robin Hawkins has been feeding animals at the Philadelphia Zoo since 1965 and has seen tons of zoo-chini devoured in his time. He has strong opinions on this topic.

Hawkins informs us, "Zoo-chini was developed in 1967 for some of our finicky zebras, and it worked well. But once we gave it to the zebras, all of the herbivores were asking for it—the goats, the koalas, the deer, and the rabbits, to name a few. And the llamas are the worst. It's like they have a union that demands that zoo-chini must be fried and flavored just right or they refuse to be friendly to our customers.

"Well, I don't have to take no drama from no llama. I've been here almost fifty years and don't need the money. I tell the llamas that they can cry to Mama, but I'm their daddy, so eat it or starve, baby."

A FINAL REVIEW

1. "My Sharia More" and "You Bin Laden on My Mind" are examples of:
   a. Talibanjo music
   b. anthropomurphism
   c. Pastafari ballads
   d. romanitarian acts
   e. none of the above

2. According to Cheryl Bitman, what should you serve a patient after recovering from hernia repair?
   a. split pea soup with pasta
   b. beef burritos and chili
   c. something pastriotic
   d. something light

3. Of the following dictators, who did not head a **turtle-itarian** regime?
   a. Mao Zedong
   b. Joseph Stalin
   c. Pol Pot
   d. Idi Amin

4. Which of the following sports did the remarkable Ludmilla Martin *not* excel at?
   a. arm wrestling
   b. ice hockey
   c. basketball
   d. indoor gymnastics
   e. wintersaults

TAKE ME OUT TO THE BALLPARK

(WITH THE BOOB BIRDS AND THE WARNING TRUCKS)

WORDAPODS INSPIRED BY OUR NATIONAL PASTIME

Around the Corn

Around the Corn (n)—in baseball, the traditional throw around the infield after an out is recorded—in games played in Iowa

Wisdom From Left Field

This kernel of baseball jargon originated from a minor league contest played on a beautiful corn-laden infield in Dubuque. As legend has it, after a runner was thrown out at first on a routine grounder, shortstop Nibby Nickerson yelled at first baseman Vern "Silky" Summers to "throw it around." "Around where?" yelled the first sacker. "Around the corn, you idiot," replied the impatient Nickerson, who had unwittingly just started a cherished Iowa baseball tradition.

This custom soon spread around the Midwest and then around baseball fields across the country. As most of the fields were corn-challenged, the expression soon changed to the more universal "around the horn."

Bingle

Bingle (n) or (v)—a bunt that goes for a single, as opposed to a sacrifice

b) (as a verb)—Osvaldo Rodriguez caught the defense napping and bingled successfully down the third-base line.

Sample Sentence: I prefer that my pitcher bunt for a sacrifice, as he always bungles his bingles.

Mastering the Word

The best time for a bingle is _____

    a. when the defense is expecting a sacrifice bunt
    b. when the defense is playing back
    c. during the seventh-inning stretch
    d. when you're craving a salty snack

Batter's Ballot Box

Batter's Ballot Box (n)—a voting machine set up between the on-deck circle and the dugout where baseball players can vote during a game

A Little Off Base

The tradition of the batter's ballot box (BBB) started in baseball-crazy St. Louis, Missouri, where a group of politically minded independent league players complained to the election board that they were scheduled to play on Election Day and had forgotten to file for absentee ballots.

The election board—thinking that it would encourage others to vote as well—came up with the idea of a batter's ballot box, which was used for several years.

You may have suspected that the BBB is a thing of the past, and you are correct. This old-fashioned voting device has been replaced (except in certain Floridian counties) with the more efficient players' voting booth, which is usually set up in the clubhouse between the lockers and the showers. It has been reliably reported that some nonvoting players tend to mistake it for a bathroom stall, and they inadvertently pull the wrong lever. Needless to say, there's a difference between doing your civic duty and doing your septic duty.

Boob Birds

Boob Birds (n)—female fans of all sports (originally, just baseball) who voice their displeasure loudly when their home team is playing poorly

Wisdom From Left Field

This term originated (where else?) in Philadelphia, which is known far and wide for its passionate, vociferous fans. While the term "boo bird" has been around forever, it is usually associated with inebriated, leather-lunged men. But not exclusively. I recently sat down with Clara Heatley, the ringleader of a group of fans that became known as the *Boob Birds*.

Matt: So Clara, how did the Boob Birds come about?

Clara: Philadelphia, as you may know, is a sports-crazy town, and we are known far and wide for our tough fans, sometimes known as "boo birds." Well, I just thought that not all Philly fans are drunk, overweight men. How about us sober, shapely ladies?

Matt: How many Boob Birds were there originally?

Clara: Originally, it was just me, Connie Greer, and Crissy Monaco. We all worked together, and after work, we sat up in the five hundred level of old Veterans Stadium for Phillies games. Our group kept building, and there were thirty-four to thirty-six of us in our heyday.

Matt: The term, "Boob Bird." Was that your idea?

Clara: No. A local sportswriter, I forget his name, called us that. He reasoned that we vented like the men but also filled out our T-shirts quite pleasingly.

Matt: Did you find the term demeaning?

Clara: Demeaning to whom exactly? Not at all. We wore our nickname and Boob Bird T-shirts with great pride. In fact, because the names of the three original Boob Birds—Clara, Connie, and Crissy—all start with "C," we even flirted with the idea of calling ourselves the Triple C Gang.

Matt: What happened?

Clara: That nickname turned out to be a bust.

Matt: Well played!

Curtsey Runner

Curtsey Runner (n)—in men's softball leagues, a pinch runner that enters the game with an effeminate bow to the other team

A Little Off Base

In my experience, men's softball leagues feature a strange combination of passionate competition and compassionate rules. For instance, many leagues use double-bags to try to reduce the number of collisions and injuries resulting from contact around first base. In some of these leagues, sliding into home is discouraged, and anyone trying to bowl over the catcher will face a penalty ranging from an ejection to a long suspension.

The courtesy runner is allowed in many leagues that recognize that players are either injured, slow as molasses, simply old, or all of the above. A player reaching base can utilize a courtesy runner and still re-enter the game defensively, or as a batter.

Of course, the curtsey runner takes such sportsmanship to an area that nobody is comfortable with, and he is an affront to whatever macho code remains in men's softball leagues.

Eastpaw

Eastpaw (n)—a pitcher who is able to pitch effectively with both his right and left arms

Wisdom From Left Field

There have been very few pitchers who were ambidextrous enough to hurl the ball well from both arms. One such pitcher who absolutely excelled from both wings was the peculiar Luigi (Lights Out) Lonergan. In 1974, Lonergan retired from the Amarillo Dillas of the United League of Baseball after posting some eye-popping numbers. But let's take a step back.

A pitcher who throws from the left side (a lefty) is called a *southpaw*, but one never hears a righty referred to as a *northpaw*. The term *eastpaw*, however, seemed to be made-to-order for Lonergan.

It was said that Lonergan could throw almost one hundred miles per hour from either wing and also possessed a great curveball and change-up. That made him hard enough to hit. What made him almost impossible to hit was his freakish delivery, one that allowed him to spin around to either side in the middle of his windup. Utilizing such talent and trickery, Luigi amassed a career record of 270 wins, 9 losses, and a miniscule 0.13 ERA.

So why is this, perhaps, your very first acquaintance with Luigi (Lights Out) Lonergan? Lonergan was a very principled man who spurned multimillion-dollar offers to pitch in the major leagues, saying that he was only in it for the "purity of the game." His attitude was not popular with his wives, all seven of whom divorced him.

Eastpaws just never get the respect they deserve.

Fungocide

Fungocide (n)—a special chemical compound that is used to instantly kill fungo bats

A Little Off Base

In the 1940s, the Pittsburgh Piranha, a minor league team, had a general manager named Rupert Spotwood. Spotwood, who would do almost anything to gain an advantage over his opponents, was nicknamed *Branch Sickey* for his unethical tactics.

One of his brainstorms was to hire a group of chemists to come up with a way to kill the visiting teams' fungo bats so they could not take infield practice before the games. Once the compound was tested to be effective, Spotwood paid a group of cops to infiltrate the other team's clubhouse and apply the fungocide to their bats.

While the fungocide seemed to work, the ploy didn't. Even without full infield practice, opponents regularly trounced the Piranha, who finished last that season. No problem! Under Branch Sickey's leadership and a variety of more time-tested, nefarious tricks, the Piranha recovered to win four out of the next five league championships.

Grand Salami

Grand Salami (or simply, Salami) (n)—slang for a grand slam, a home run hit with the bases loaded, scoring four total runs

Wisdom From Left Field

Little Stevie Peppenstein was a light-hitting, smooth-fielding reserve shortstop for the New York Giants of the 1900s. Stevie was not only a slick fielder but was said to be pretty slick with the ladies as well.

On August 5, 1907, Peppenstein, who at the time hadn't hit a major league home run in five years, came to the plate in the bottom of the tenth inning with the bases full and his team down by three runs to the Pittsburgh Pirates. Well, you know what happened next. On a full count, Stevie connected like never before and blasted the ball over the left field wall to win the game.

In the jubilation that followed, his excited manager said, "That wasn't merely a grand slam; that was a grand salami!" Stevie, no stranger to playing hide-the-salami with his female admirers, replied, "Well, in that case, Skip, it's the first time I've intentionally shown my salami in public."

Good ol' Salami Steve.

The Hot Coroner

The Hot Coroner (n)—the original moniker given to the third-base position

A Little Off Base

Back in the days before the Rockford Peaches played in a league of their own, there were quite a few co-ed baseball leagues that stipulated that at least two players in the field must be women.

Enter the beautiful and highly skilled Lila Lovicki, who would've started at third for any team in the league, whether or not they had the two-women rule. The lovely Lila, a former beauty queen, worked in the county coroner's office by day and made every play at third base by night. Well known for her day job, she also became so proficient at her night job that opposing managers would instruct their hitters, "Hey, don't hit the ball to that hot coroner over there."

The phrase stuck to her as naturally as line drives stuck to the webbing of her mitt, and soon all third basemen were said to man (or woman) the hot coroner. Over time, it simply became the *hot corner.*

Kiddush Cup

Kiddush Cup (n)—a cup-shaped protective device worn in the jockstrap by young, observant Jewish ballplayers

Wisdom From Left Field

The wearing of the kiddush cup was attributed to a devout Jew and great young power-hitting catcher named Moe Foxberg. Fearing that a Friday afternoon game would end past the start of the Sabbath, Foxberg designed a plastic cup that was both protective and sacramental in nature.

Although the game ended in time for him to get home for the start of Shabbat, Foxberg took a ceremonial swig of wine from his cup before walking home to be with his family. In later years, torn between a career as a rabbi or as a ballplayer, Foxberg chose the obvious route. He became a personal injury attorney.

Round Tripper

Round Tripper (n)—one of many nicknames given to a home run in baseball—with a fascinating story behind it

A Little Off Base

Horrid Horace Henderson was a clumsy oaf of a first baseman who played mostly independent league baseball in or around Galveston, Texas, in the 1920s. Henderson stood 5'7" and weighed about 265 on days when he remembered to diet. Henderson could flat-out powder a baseball, but he couldn't field a lick, and his managers (with no designated hitter rule to fall back on) would try to hide him at first base.

Horrid Horace was a lousy fielder and inept base runner who would regularly trip while waddling around the bases. So why did he earn a spot in the lineup? The big man hit about fifty home runs every season!

Legend has it that after one of his majestic blasts, Henderson went into his home run trot and tripped over second base. While he was recovering from the face plant, a fan yelled from the stands, "Down goes the Round Tripper!"

The nickname stuck, and "round tripper" was soon applied to any of his home runs and, to this day, to a home run hit by any player—whether or not he does a pratfall on his home run trot.

Rubber Game

Rubber Game (n)—the deciding game of a series in any sport, especially baseball, basketball, and hockey

Wisdom From Left Field

The term *rubber game* goes back to the days when condoms could only be obtained on the black market. Many players enjoyed amorous adventures with their admirers off the field, but their only form of protection they had access to was a jockstrap and cup. With both items kind of defeating the purpose, one can clearly imagine that rubbers were a greatly prized item circa 1895 or so.

Before a hotly contested championship game between Cincinnati and Detroit, a local entrepreneur named Duffy Wallbanger offered all players on the winning team a box of condoms. With both teams playing at a fevered pitch, Detroit pulled out (pun intended) a 10–9 victory in a then-record twenty-three innings. Ironically, most of the winning players were too exhausted from the marathon game to enjoy the fruits of their labor for another day or so.

Rue-Barb

Rue-Barb (n)—a very strange baseball tradition of the past where, as part of the seventh-inning stretch, all fans were encouraged to stand up and rue the fact that they ever had met someone named Barbara

A Little Off Base

Okay, here's the story behind it. Stubby Herring, the owner of the Freehold Flashers, was embroiled in a nasty public custody battle with his ex-wife, Barbara. Seizing the microphone from the PA announcer just before the traditional singing of "Take Me Out to the Ballgame," Herring unleashed a ten-minute tirade against Barbara and encouraged everyone in the crowd to either rip Barb Herring or, absent that, any other Barb they might know.

When he finished venting his spleen, the owner got a standing ovation, and the tradition (albeit in much shorter tirades) continued in Freehold and in other minor league stadiums in New Jersey for a few more seasons.

Subway Pitch

Subway Pitch (n)—similar to a submarine pitch, a pitch thrown from a position between sidearm and underhand

b) in modern usage, a pitch thrown with a sidearm or underarm motion in a game played between the Yankees and Mets

Wisdom From Left Field

In baseball history, there have been quite a few successful pitchers who baffled batters with their strange "submarine" pitch. The first known practitioner of this type of pitch was Snuffy Shilovitz—who captained a submarine during World War II. A baseball fanatic who dreamed of playing in the Major Leagues before and after performing his duty for his country, Snuffy was said to possess a great, traditional, over-the-top fastball before he entered the service.

Due to the constraints of being on a submarine, he used to practice throwing an almost underhand motion in informal games of catch with his shipmates. He became so adept at this style of pitching that he brought it with him to his audition with the St Louis Cardinals in 1945. When he threw batting practice that day, even the legendary Stan Musial couldn't hit him. Musial was said to have uttered this famous line after whiffing against Snuffy—"I can't even lay wood on his subway balls, and I'm the freakin' Man!"

The rest of his story is bathed in mystery. As legend has it, within sniffing distance of making the Cards roster, poor Snuffy went out trout fishing and came home with some kind of devastating injury. Alas, Shilovitz never pitched again, but his subway pitch did see some success in the bigs.

Suicide Sneeze

Suicide Sneeze (n)—an unusual play in which the batter intentionally sneezes forcibly, thereby distracting the pitcher and catcher and allowing the runner to score from third base

A Little Off Base

The most noted practitioner of the suicide sneeze play was a minor leaguer named Hippalito "Nosey" Perez, who was said to have the largest honker in the Venezuelan League. Perez was so adept at this tactic that he pulled off fifty successful suicide sneeze plays in his minor league career. Sadly, he was also a career .143 hitter (and a mediocre fielder to boot) who never got called up to the major leagues.

Please Note: While the sneeze has been a literal part of the suicide sneeze over the years, thankfully, the suicide part has not been.

Warning Truck

Warning Truck (n)—in certain baseball stadiums, a truck that is placed in the outfield a few feet in front of the home run fence

Wisdom From Left Field

Of all the stupid baseball innovations—and there have been more than a few—this has to take the cake for the most asinine, or if you will, **asiten** (please see entry) of them all.

Johnny "Little Cheese" Gambino, owner of both Gambino Trucking and the Waterloo (Ohio) Wildcats, thought that his innovation would add some drama to long fly balls and also increase exposure for his company.

The owner instructed the team's grounds crew to place a large eighteen-wheeler with "Gambino Trucking" prominently displayed in red letters about ten feet in front of the center field fence. The novelty seemed to cause a buzz in the stadium, and the experiment appeared to be on its way to success when in the seventh inning, center fielder Pedro Rosario went crashing through the windshield to rob a hitter of extra bases.

Rosario lay motionless on the field for twenty minutes, during which time Johnny Gambino himself drove the truck off the field to a serenade of boos. Little Cheese, quite devastated by the result of his greed and stupidity, sold the team one week later and also dissolved his trucking business. He went on to achieve infamy as a foreign policy advisor in the Bush (II) administration.

And what of Pedro Rosario? Rosario was never the same after his collision with the warning truck, and he (successfully) sued the owner for ending his once-promising baseball career. He became a record producer and even penned and sang a top-selling blues-rock-salsa hit called "I Got Warning Truck Power, Baby."

REVIEWING THE REVIEWS

REVIEW OF FIRST FIFTY

1. barkolepsy
2. Barry White-fish Salad
3. biknockerlars (a couple of the other choices were also tempting)
4. a and b only (ass-steroids often increase productivity, at least in the short-term)

FIRST 101 WORDAPODS REVIEW

Jason would be considered by most to be a nice guy, but he was also a single guy who felt a need for female companionship, and he was not the type to pay for it. One evening he took a colleague out to dinner, but she enjoyed her food a little too much for his liking. Jason suspected that she was into **feastiality**. They decided to become friends, and she planned to attend his next concert, where he would proudly play his **clockenspiel** while she would refrain from eating too noticeably.

So where would he find his next girlfriend? Jason pondered this as he sipped at his horrible cup of **brewp.** (Although ravenous, as he was wearing his **hungarees**, he wasn't hungry enough to enjoy *that* concoction.) None of his African American friends invited him over for a **Barry White-fish salad,** and he didn't want to go to a poetry reading, where there were likely to be some **haikugars** in attendance.

Jason studied his shopping list, acknowledging that he would try to meet some ladies at the meat market. He left his house for the market, also bringing his **grossery** list just in case. What else would he need?

Well, he reasoned, he could discreetly scout women in the distant aisles, so he also brought along a pair of **biknockerlars.**

In the produce aisle, Jason spotted a biker-babe-type, who was wearing a **bananadanna**. Trying to impress her, he started to juggle some potatoes. "That takes some **imashination**," Donna said with a smile. Jason started to talk to her but found out that they had very little in common. They didn't even like the same foods; Jason preferred fish, and Donna was something of a **carnibore**. They wished each other well, and Jason even offered to take her out for a nice, refreshing **bilkshake** at the custard stand.

Jason pushed his cart down the aisles, pretending to fill up the basket, but there were very few ladies in the market. Oh, he did almost hurt his neck when he **blubbernecked** to see a five-hundred-pound man, but that was not why he came. Resigned to packing it in for the day, Jason made one more loop around the store. From a distance, he spotted a woman with a beautiful body in aisle fifteen. Was this the break he needed, or was it simply a **fakethrough** of sorts?

Jason, no Brad Pitt himself, wheeled over to aisle fifteen, beholding the stranger's beautiful body, but he did not find her to be that good-looking. "She's more like a **knocker spaniel**," he thought. He gave her a shy wave, even as the woman was thinking that she would rather be subject to a **conventory** than go out with someone like him.

Returning home, Jason searched the fridge for some **lefties**. He ate up everything he could find, and feeling bored, he started walking to a nearby **boredello**—a place where he would pay a little bit to be rewarded with a good night's sleep.

REVIEW OF FIRST 150

1. all of the above
2. all of the above hyphenated tactics
3. the manituba
4. everything from soup to nuts (give yourself half-credit if you went with *a prudent sampling of Danish*)

POP QUIZ: THE FIRST 200

1. False (tricky, huh?)
2. pastriotic
3. lemmings (lots of followers)
4. misconstrudel
5. his pinochle sandwiches
6. True—absolutely (or, so I've heard)
7. vivid imashination
8. both are overpriced
9. more than 1,200 (1,238)
10. This book will sell millions. (Harry will get around to it; have faith!)

A FINAL REVIEW

1. Talibanjo music
2. something light
3. Joseph Stalin (he moved too quickly)
4. indoor gymnastics

One-on-One with Dr. Marta Hari

Dr. Marta Hari has built a thriving psychology practice in her adopted hometown of Funkstown, Maryland. Author of the clinical classic *Young Head Cases*, she is a frequent guest on many talk shows and may also be seen on a few popular infomercials. Marta is not only well known for her imposing intellect and take-no-prisoners approach to family counseling; she is also very beautiful and is quite aware of the spell she casts on her male patients. I arrived at her stylish office with a mixture of anticipation and trepidation. Call it *anticidation*. Below is the transcript from our first interview.

Matt: Dr. Hari, I first want to thank you for your invaluable help with my book. And may I add that you are even more stunning in person?

Marta: Yes, you may. But what do you mean by *invaluable?* It connotes the opposite of *valuable*, although a synonym. You could have just said *valuable,* or *estimable.* Even *priceless* would have been preferable. Don't you think?

Matt: Come to think of it, I do. My thoughts exactly. It was as if you were—

Marta: Reading your mind.

Matt: Yes.

Marta: It's what I do. Why don't you unburden yourself on that comfy sofa over there?

Matt: Oh, the one with the nice **Freudian slipcover** (please see entry) under your portrait?

Marta: That's the one. Please be seated.

Matt: Thank you. Dr. Hari—

Marta: Marta.

Matt: Marta. Can you tell my readers how long you have been practicing psychology?

Marta: How many readers do you have?

Matt: Millions—hopefully.

Marta: A few years or so. About twenty. Do I look good for my age?

Matt: Certainly. For any age.

Marta: Are you trying to flatter me?

Matt: Yes. I mean *no.* I mean I just wanted to tell the truth.

Marta: Do I make you nervous?

Matt: Sometimes.

Marta: But you just met me.

Matt: Okay, every time I've met you, I've been nervous. But over the phone—

Marta: You weren't nervous at all?

Matt: No. Not really.

Marta: So pretend we're talking over the phone.

Matt: Hello. Hello? This is Matt. Who's calling, please?

Marta: Charming. So when did you get the idea for this book? Do you think that it's necessary?

Matt: Well, I think that this idea has been percolating for a number of years.

Marta: What number?

Matt: Number of what?

Marta: For how many years has this idea for a collection of interesting words been percolating before it bubbled to the surface?

Matt: It's hard to assign an exact number of years, and I don't know if my readers need to know that.

Marta: Should I end our session now?

Matt: No, not yet. I think the idea has been there for about seventeen years, but I just now had—

Marta: The courage, temerity, and vision to write and publish it?

Matt: Well, yes. I'm not sure about the temerity part, but I like "courage and vision."

Marta: I thought I'd throw you a bone. All of you—

Matt: Dogs?

Marta: Need a bone every now and then.

Matt: Thank you.

Marta: So why did it take you so long?

Matt: I don't know. I was just waiting for—

Marta: A time when you'd be older and less energetic.

Matt: Hey, I'm very young and energetic, as far as my readers are concerned.

Marta: And you have lots of readers?

Matt: I'm working on it. Will you help me spread the word?

Marta: I could buy a few copies under consignment.

Matt: You know a ton of people. Is that the best you can do?

Marta: Probably. So why do you think all of us need to learn these interesting words and phrases?

Matt: Wordapods.

Marta: You may want to change the title.

Matt: You don't like the title, *Wordapodia,* and, and, *wordapods?*

Marta: I didn't say I didn't like the title. I said, "*You* may want to change the title."

Matt: I do. How did you know that?

Marta: I'm a brilliant psychologist. Remember?

Matt: That's right. I knew I was here for a reason.

Marta: Reasons. Many reasons. But our time is just about over for today.

Matt: I feel better already.

Marta: Thank you, but we're just getting started. To totally unblock your fear of beautiful psychologists and to free you of your long-manifested symptoms of Stunted Creativity Syndrome, I suggest a minimum of five more appointments. No, that won't do it. I suggest we meet for at least fifteen more sessions.

Matt: Thank you, I think. May I ask you a question?

Marta: Sure. Why not?

Matt: May I ask *you* the questions next time and consider our sessions to be interviews for my book?

Marta: No, I think you have enough material for now. Here's a little homework assignment for next time. Please think about whether or not you were a precocious child.

Matt: Well, I don't know. I was a premature baby, but I'm not sure—

Marta: There is very little, if any, correlation between premature birth and precocious behavior. In fact, many premature babies are known for their postcocious development.

Matt: Is *postcocious* really a word? May I use that in my book?

Marta: No, I think it's too late for this volume. Maybe next time. Oh, and please see Bianca in billing. You do have insurance, right? Thank you for enabling me to treat you. Bianca also schedules my appointments.

Manufactured By: RR Donnelley
                    Breinigsville, PA USA
                    September, 2010